AF473880

THE SPITFIRE

Published by IWM, Lambeth Road, London SE1 6HZ
iwm.org.uk

ISBN 978-1-912423-43-9

A catalogue record for this book is available from the British Library.
Printed and bound by Gomer Press Limited
Colour reproduction by DL Imaging

Front cover: Spitfire Mk VB, R6923 'QJ-S', of 92 Squadron based at Biggin Hill, Kent, May 1941.

Back cover: Spitfire Mk VC's of 2 Squadron South African Air Force (SAAF) based at Palata, Italy, flying over the Adriatic Sea while on a bombing mission, November 1943.

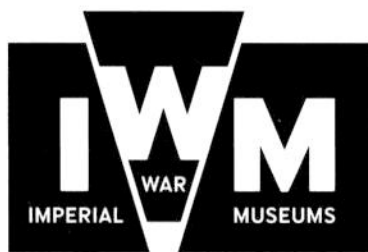

THE SPITFIRE

Adrian Kerrison

INTRODUCTION

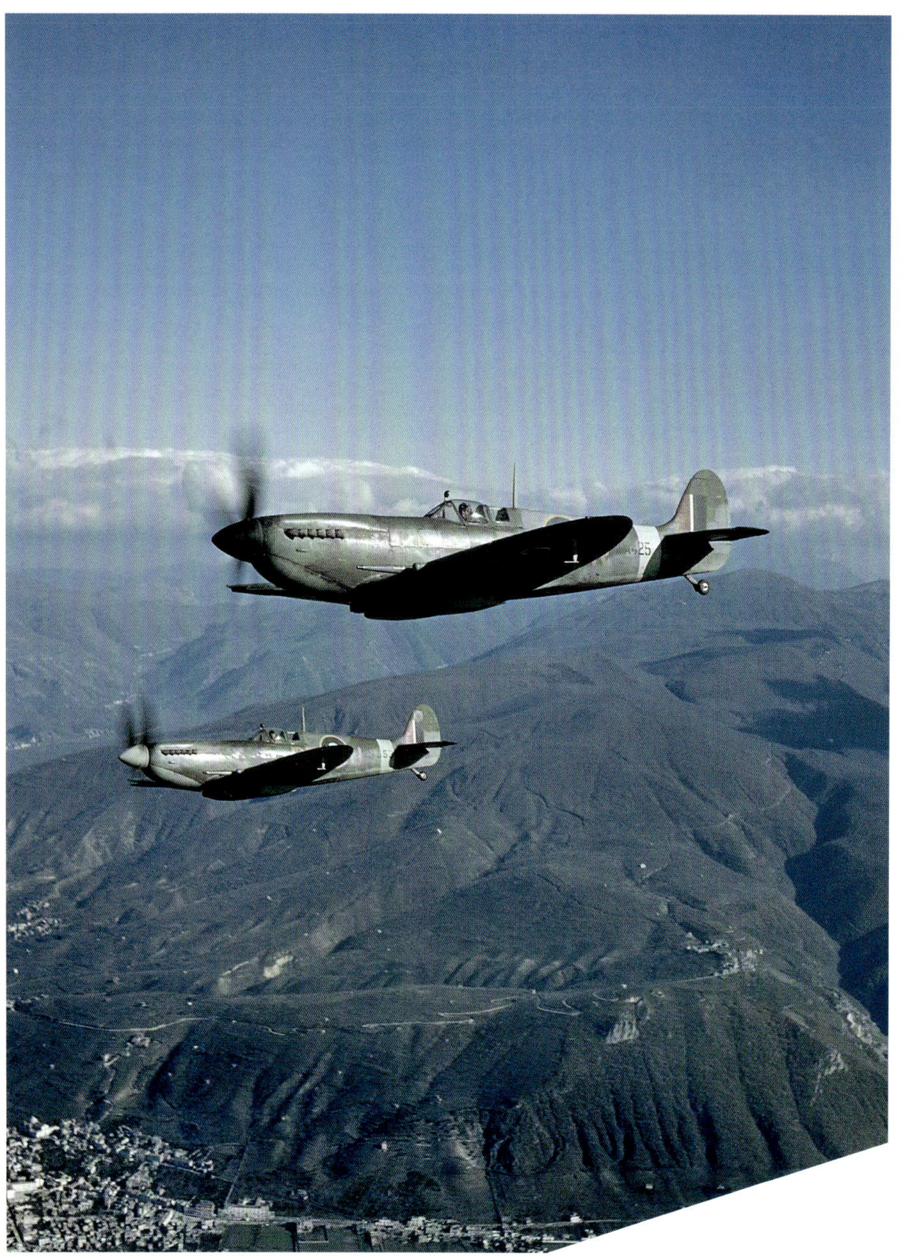

Two Spitfire Mk IX's of 241 Squadron, MA425 'RZ-R' and MH635 'RZ-U', flying over mountainous country south of Rome, January 1944 (crop).

Icon. Legend. Saviour.

These are just a few words that have been used to describe the Supermarine Spitfire in the more than 85 years since its first flight in March 1936.

From the heroic role it played against the Luftwaffe in the Battle of Britain to its present-day status as a firm air show favourite, the Spitfire has achieved an almost mythical status in the public imagination. With much of its allure stemming from its easily recognisable, aesthetically pleasing design, characterised by thin elliptical wings and gentle curves, the Spitfire's significance perhaps lies more in its abilities and track record as an exceptional fighting machine that saw it become a symbol of Britain and the Commonwealth's resistance and ultimate victory in the Second World War.

Designed by Reginald J Mitchell of Supermarine Aviation, the cutting-edge monoplane fighter was originally developed as a daytime interceptor, intended to defend the skies of Britain from enemy air attack. The Spitfire was first introduced into Royal Air Force service in August 1938 when it was issued to 19 Squadron at RAF Duxford and went on to perform its interceptor role to great effect during the Battle of Britain two years later.

The first production Spitfires were powered by Rolls Royce Merlin engines and armed with eight .303-inch machine guns. Capable of flying at speeds of up to 367mph, the Spitfire Mk I was considerably faster than the Royal Air Force (RAF)'s other single-seat fighter, the Hawker Hurricane, but more importantly matched and arguably exceeded the performance of its main opponent in 1940, Germany's Messerschmitt Bf 109.

Continuously improved and refined under the leadership of Mitchell's successor Joseph Smith, the Spitfire progressively grew more powerful and more heavily armed, allowing it to take on a variety of other roles ranging from high-speed photo reconnaissance to ground attack. By the end of its service life in the 1950s, 24 'marks' – or variants – had been designed, as well as several more sub-variants (although not all designs went into production). The final Spitfire mark, the Mk 24, was nearly 90mph faster than the first mark, despite being 2,000lbs heavier, and could climb nearly twice as fast, fly 9,000 feet higher and 140 miles further. Because it was always kept at or near the cutting edge, the Spitfire had the distinction of being the only British fighter to remain in production for the entirety of the Second World War as well as becoming the most-produced British aircraft of all time, an incredible testament to Mitchell's core design and Smith's ability to exploit it to its maximum potential.

Drawn from the IWM's world-renowned photographic collection, this book follows the Spitfire's progress from the first prototype flown in March 1936 to the last production variants flown by the RAF in the 1950s. These photographs show both the gradual as well as the dramatic changes made to the Spitfire over its decade of evolution, changes that allowed the Spitfire to fly faster, higher and farther while carrying heavier and more destructive weaponry, helping it to maintain its edge over the enemy. They show the Spitfire in the skies and airfields of Britain, Europe, the Middle East and Burma, in solitude and in formation, on the defensive and on the offensive.

Many of the photographs will be familiar, while some have been seldom seen until now. Grouped by mark, they appear in the order of when that mark went into production, which was not always sequential (for example, the Mk IX went into production before the Mk VIII). The exception to this is the PR Mk XIX, which is placed at the end in recognition of its distinction as being the variant that flew the final RAF Spitfire operation in 1954.

Some marks appear more than others, while not every mark and sub-variant could be featured. The IWM's collection of photographs featuring Spitfires mirrors Spitfire production numbers. Certain marks such as the V and the IX feature heavily in the photography collection, which makes sense as together they made up more than 60 per cent of the 20,000 plus Spitfires produced and saw service in very large numbers. In contrast, photographs of the final marks – the 21, 22 and 24 – are few and far between, a reflection of the fact that less than 500 were built and that only the Mk 21 saw limited service in the Second World War. Finally, this book does not cover the Supermarine Seafire, the carrier-borne Spitfire variant, nor does it cover Spitfires that served in foreign air forces.

The Spitfire is a tribute to the those who were involved in cementing this aircraft's place in history as one of the most legendary of all time. It is a tribute to Reginald Mitchell and Joseph Smith, their team of designers and engineers, and those at Rolls Royce who led the parallel development of the Merlin and Griffon engines. To the men and women who built the Spitfire, sometimes as enemy bombs were falling. To the ground crew who serviced the Spitfire, often in hostile and dangerous conditions, ensuring it was fit to fly. And, of course, to the pilots – many of whom became legends themselves flying the Spitfire, and many of whose last moments were at the controls of this elegant, formidable machine.

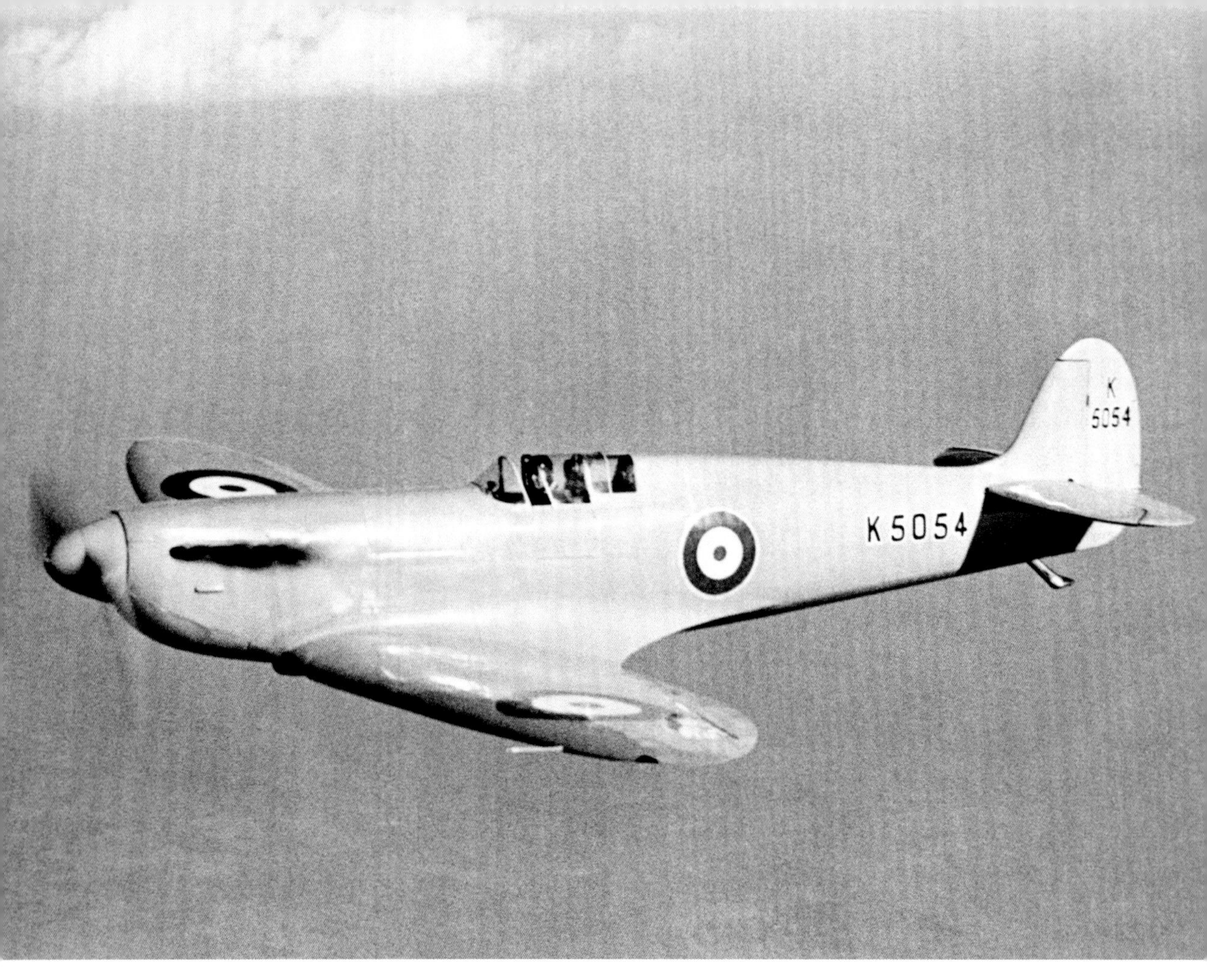
K5054
K
5054

The first Supermarine Spitfire in flight. Spitfire prototype F37/34 (serial K5054), pictured here, was first flown on 5 March 1936 by Supermarine's Chief Test Pilot Joseph 'Mutt' Summers. Three months later, the Air Ministry placed its first order for 310 Spitfires.

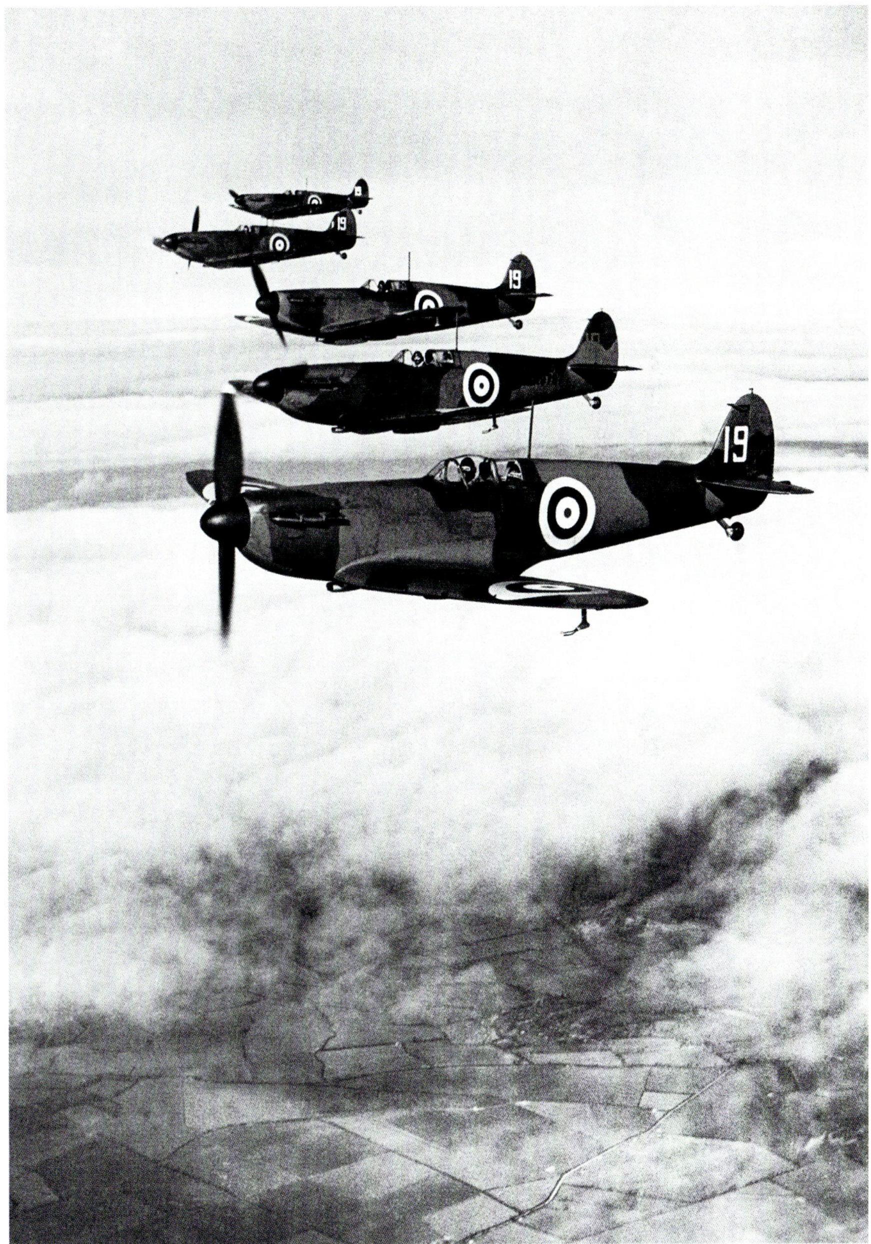

Early production Spitfire Mk I's of 19 Squadron flying in formation, October 1938. 19 Squadron was the first RAF squadron to receive the Mk I two months earlier, in August 1938. Its pilots carried out trials that were crucial in ensuring the new fighter was ready for war.

Spitfire Mk I's of 19 Squadron on display for the press at RAF Duxford in May 1939. Early production Mk I's were powered by the Rolls Royce Merlin II engine driving a fixed pitch two-bladed wooden propeller. Many also featured flat canopies, which were problematic for taller pilots.

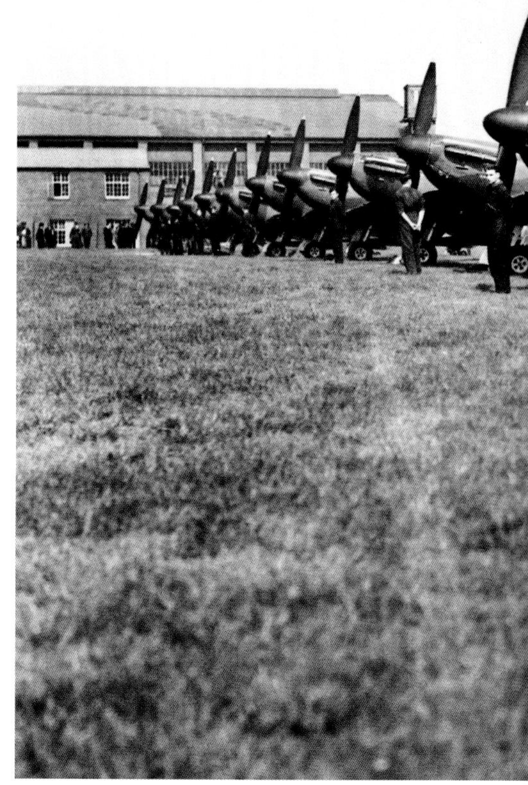

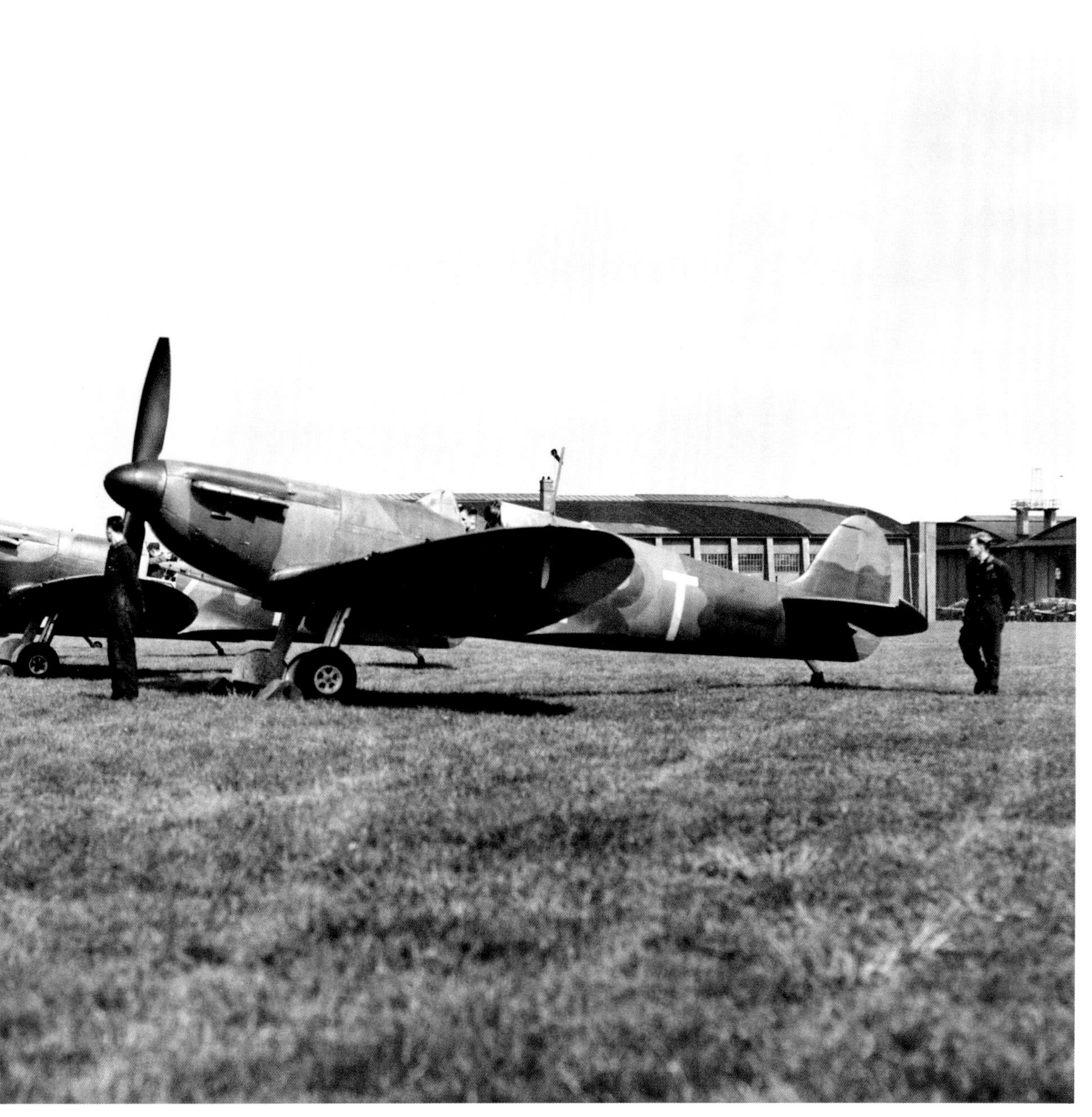

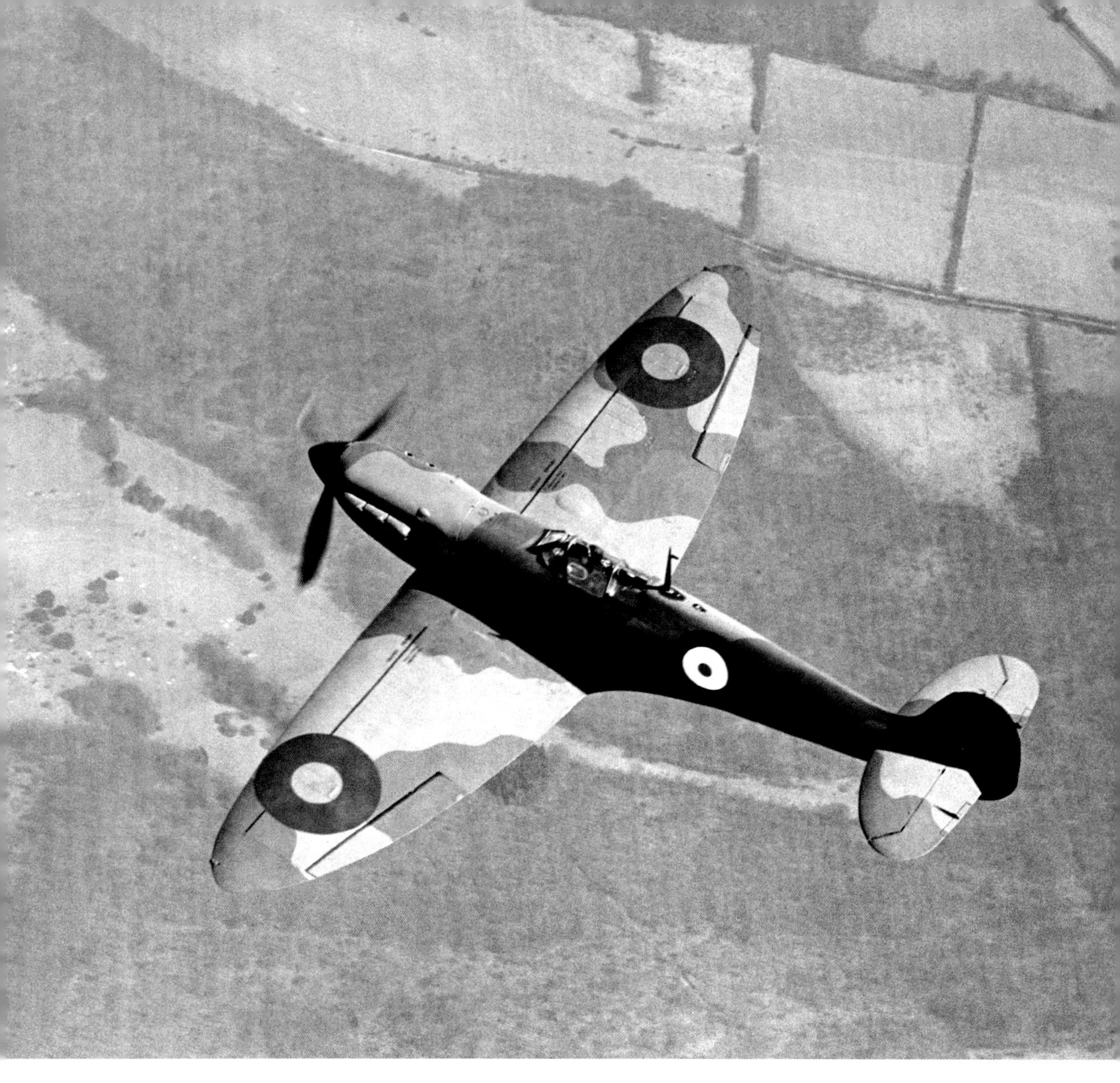

Spitfire Mk I P9450 on a test flight, April 1940. The performance of the Mk I was further improved when it was fitted with the Merlin III engine and a three-bladed variable pitch metal propeller. A 'bubble' canopy and bulletproof windscreen provided added headroom and protection for the pilot.

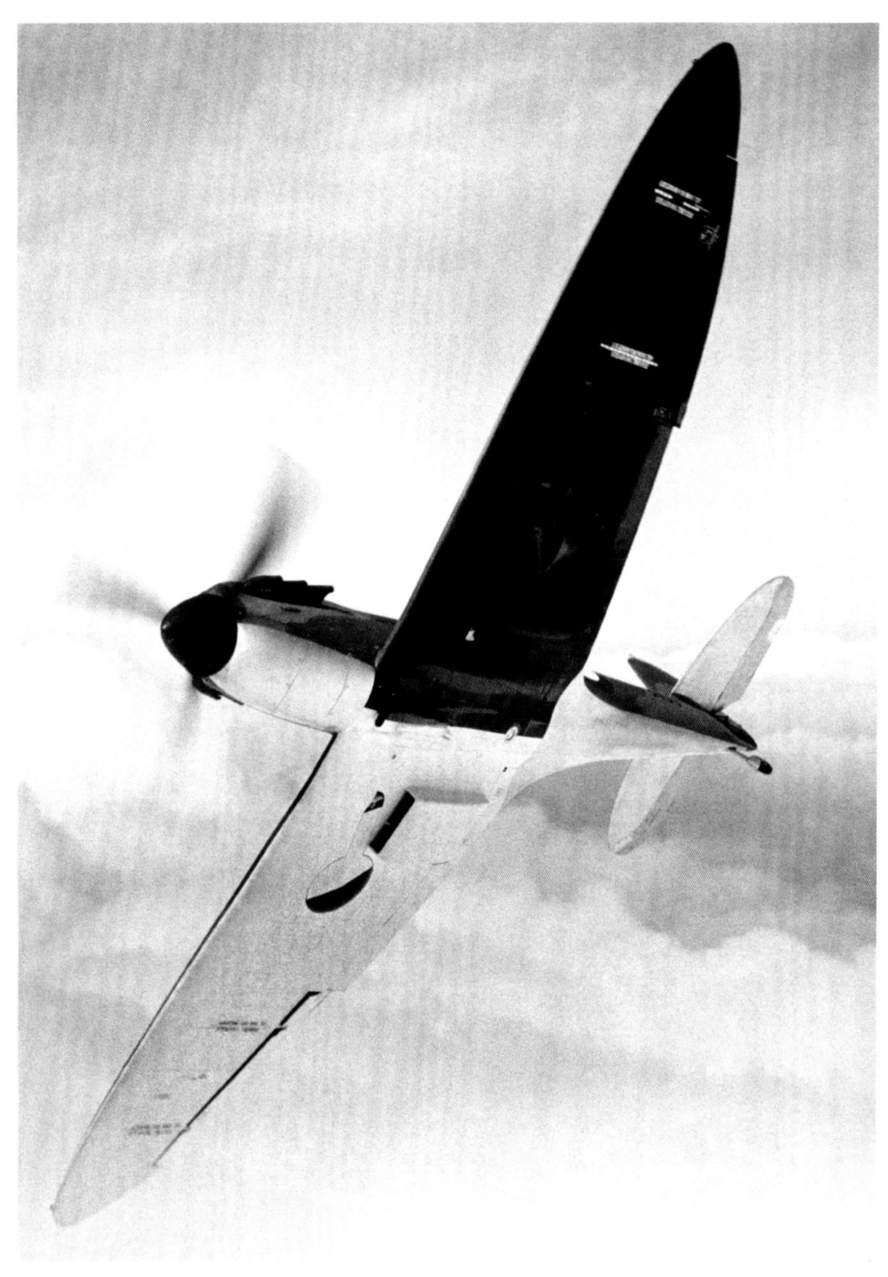

Spitfire Mk I P9450 in flight, underside view, April 1940. The Mk I was armed with eight .303 inch Browning machine guns. It first used these against the enemy on 16 October 1939 when Mk I's of 602 and 603 Squadrons intercepted German bombers attacking the Firth of Forth.

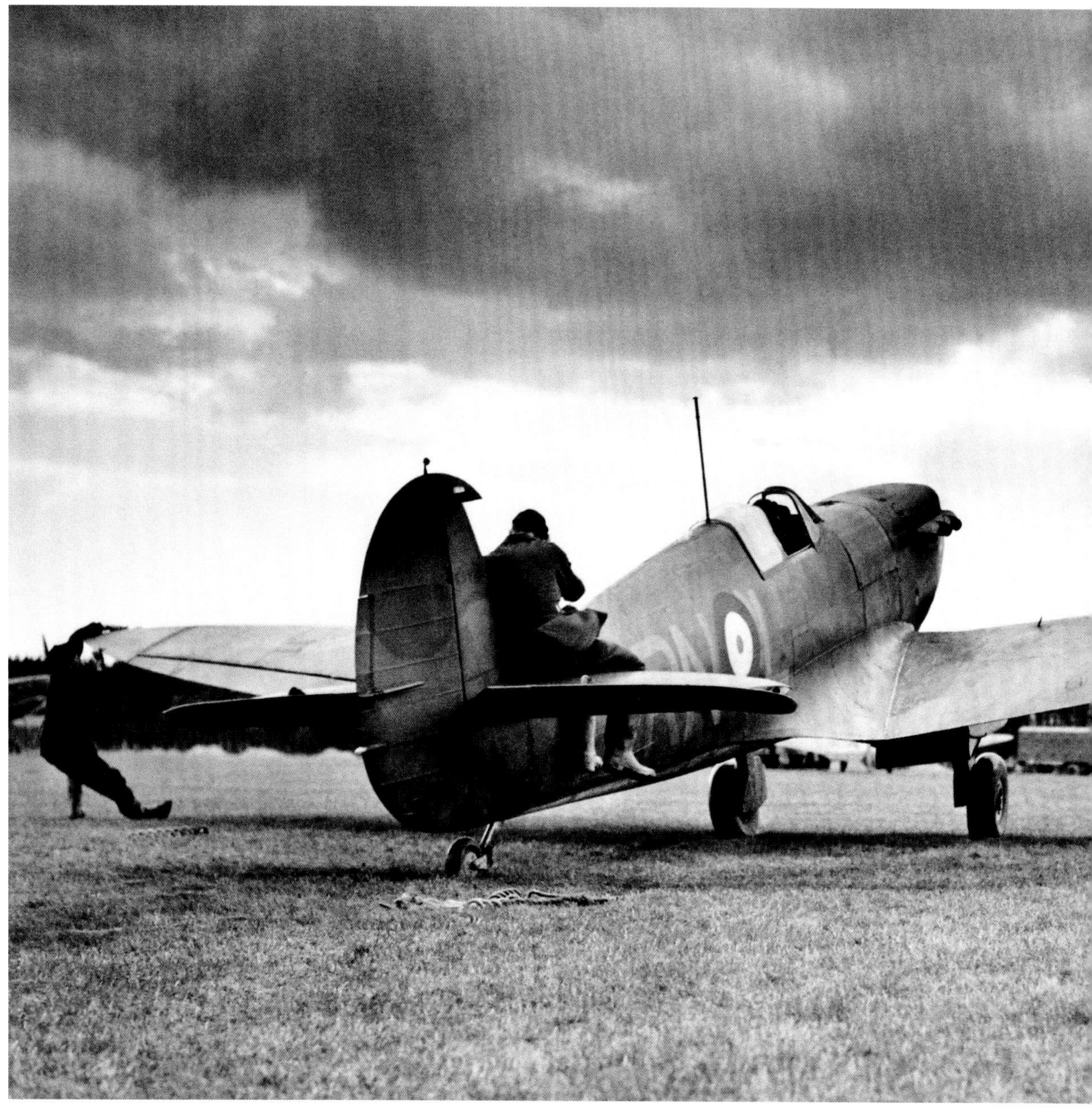

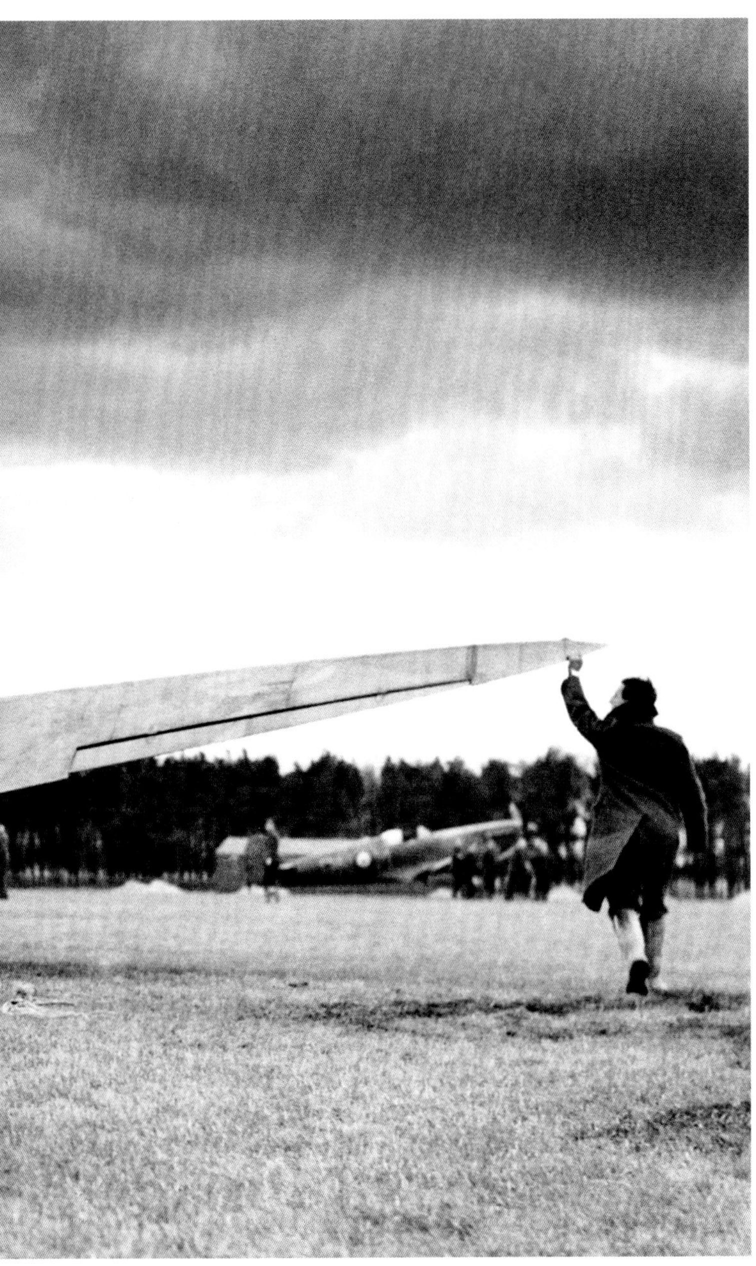

Ground crew assist a Spitfire Mk I of 72 Squadron taxiing from its dispersal at Acklington, April 1940. A month later, many Spitfire squadrons – including 72 Squadron – would get their first taste of major aerial combat while providing air cover for the Dunkirk evacuations.

Spitfire Mk I of 19 Squadron being re-armed between sorties at Fowlmere, near Duxford, September 1940. 19 Squadron were chosen to trial variants of the Mk I that were armed with more destructive 20mm Hispano cannon. Although initially unsucccessful, this paved the way for later cannon-armed Spitfires.

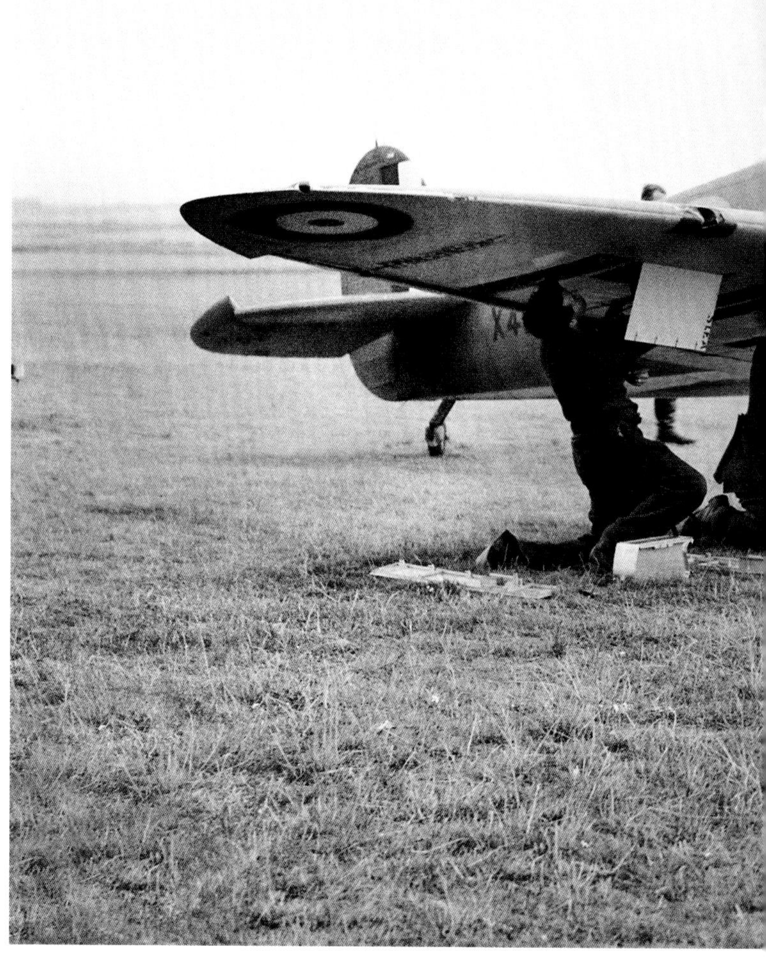

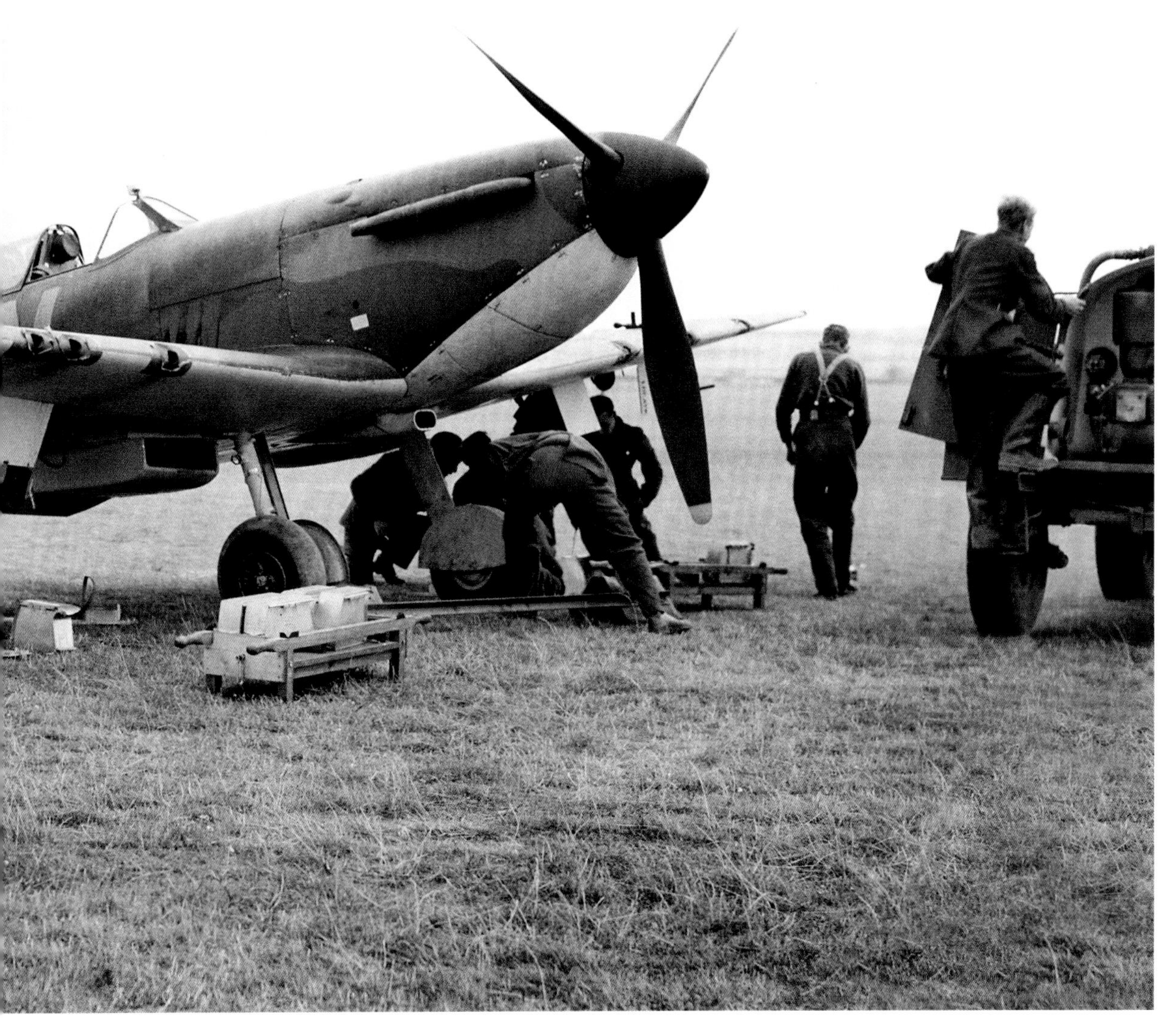

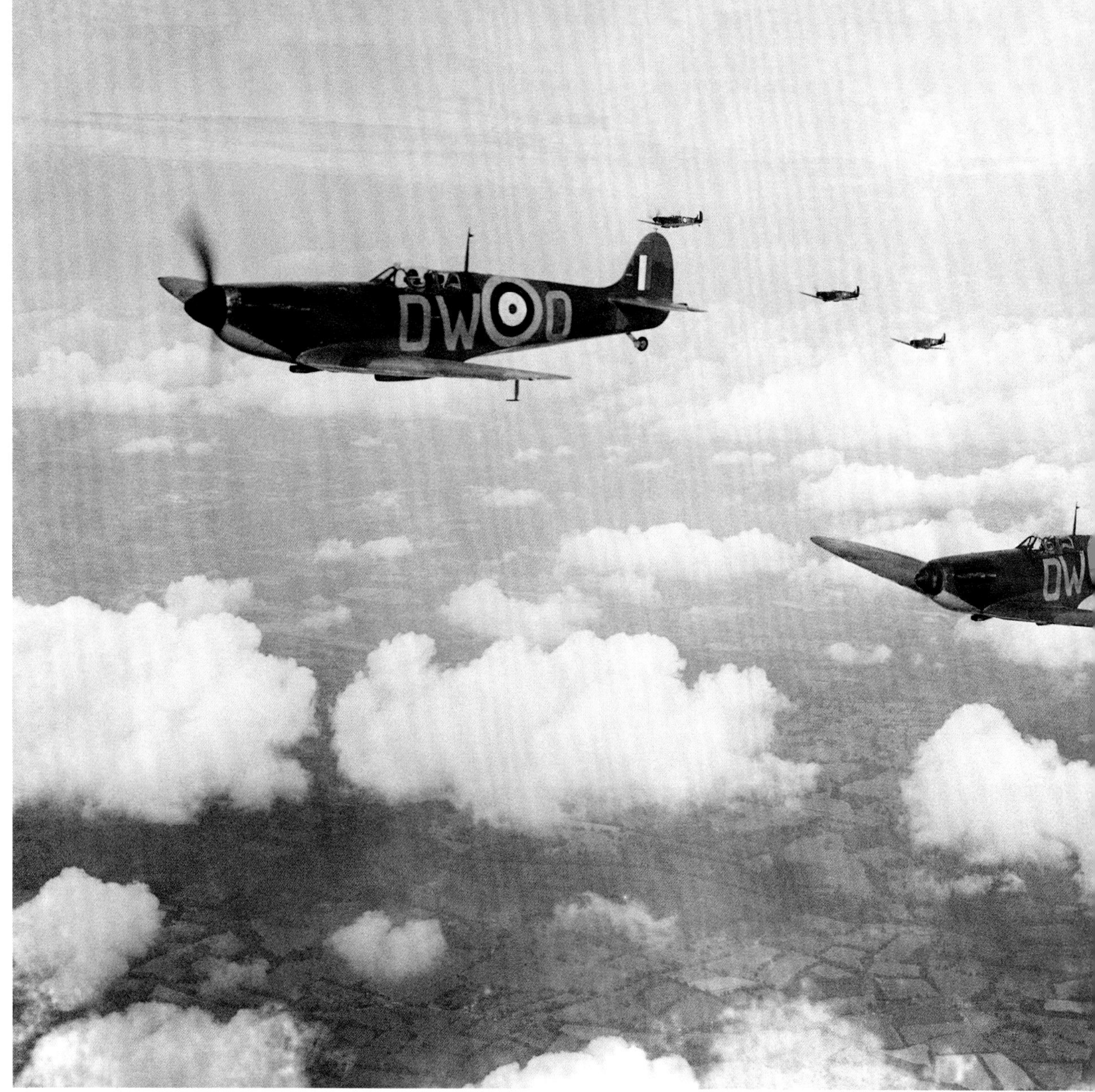
DW D
DW

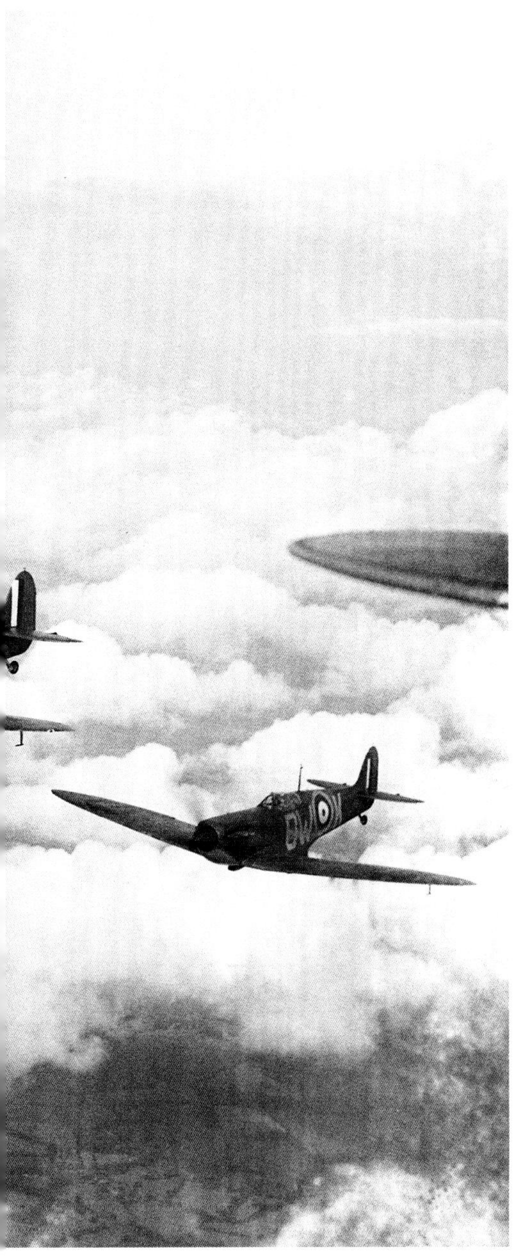

Spitfire Mk I's of 610 Squadron, based at Biggin Hill, flying in formation, July 1940. During the Battle of Britain, Spitfire squadrons were outnumbered by Hurricane squadrons three to two, but ended the battle with a better 'kill ratio' than their Hawker counterparts.

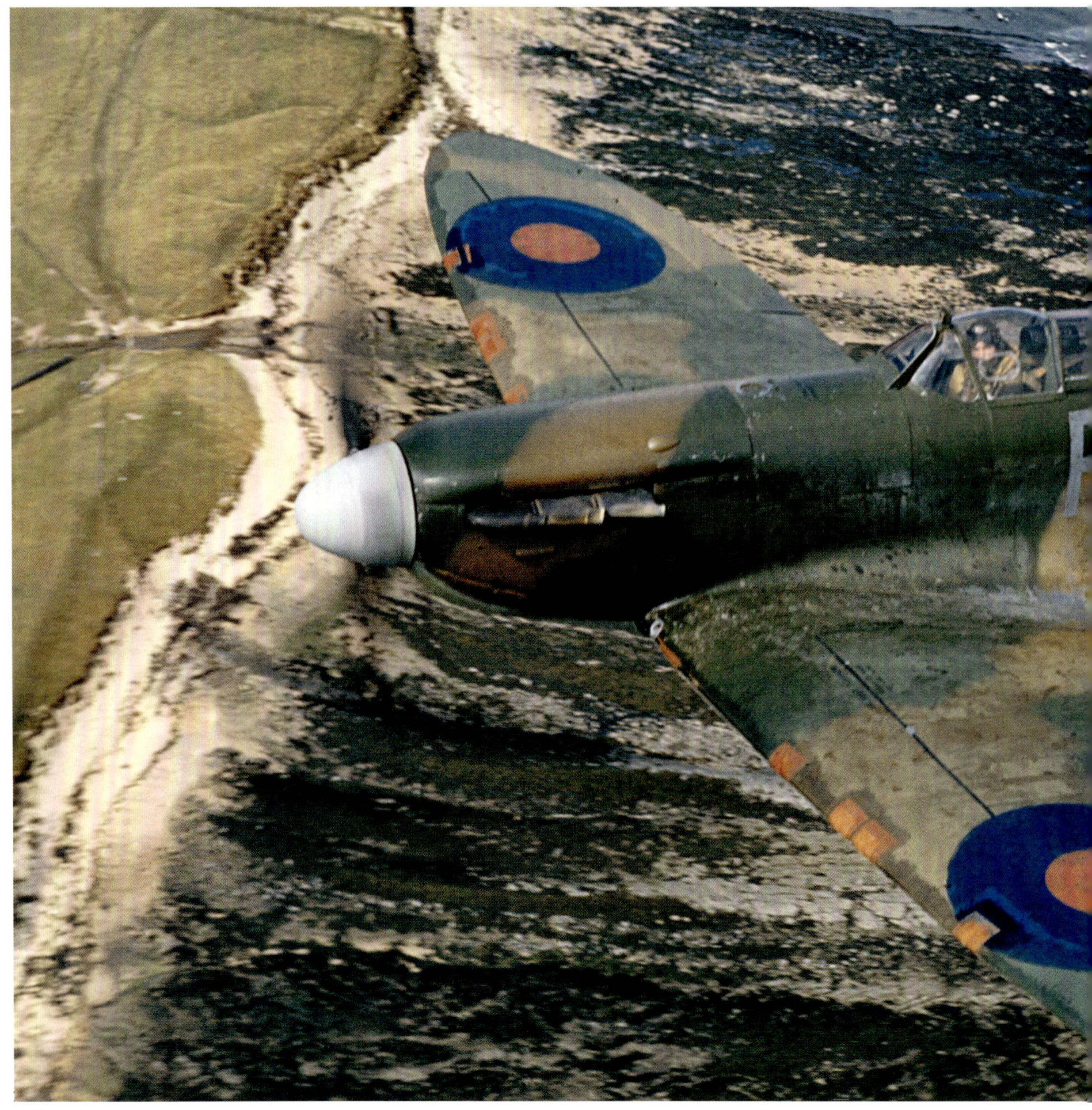

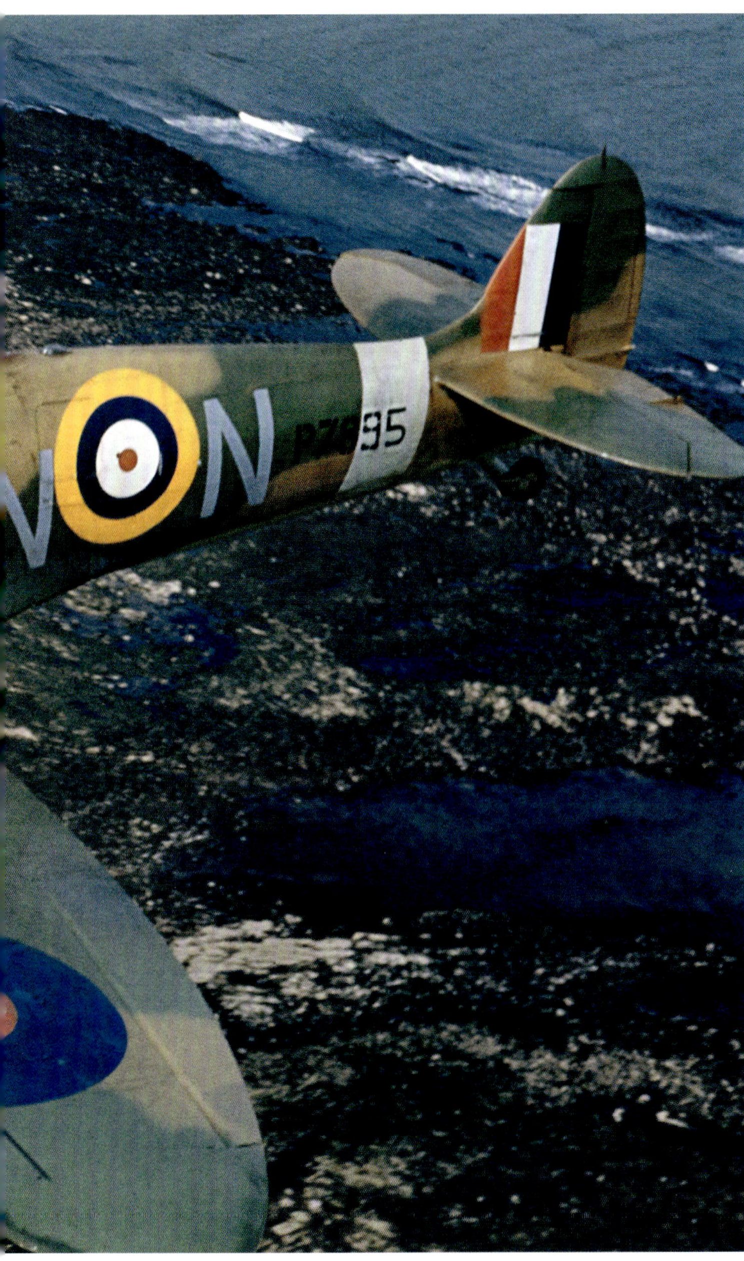

Spitfire Mk IIA, P7895 'RN-N', of 72 Squadron, based at Acklington, Northumberland, in flight over the coast in April 1941. The main improvement over the Mk I was the new Merlin XII engine paired with the Rotol or De Havilland constant speed propeller, providing an increased rate of climb and higher service ceiling.

Twelve Spitfire Mk IIA's of 72 Squadron flying in formation, 1941. The Mk II was the first Spitfire mark to be produced exclusively at the Castle Bromwich Aircraft Factory (CBAF), with 920 Mk II's built. CBAF went on to build more than half of the total 20,000-plus Spitfires produced.

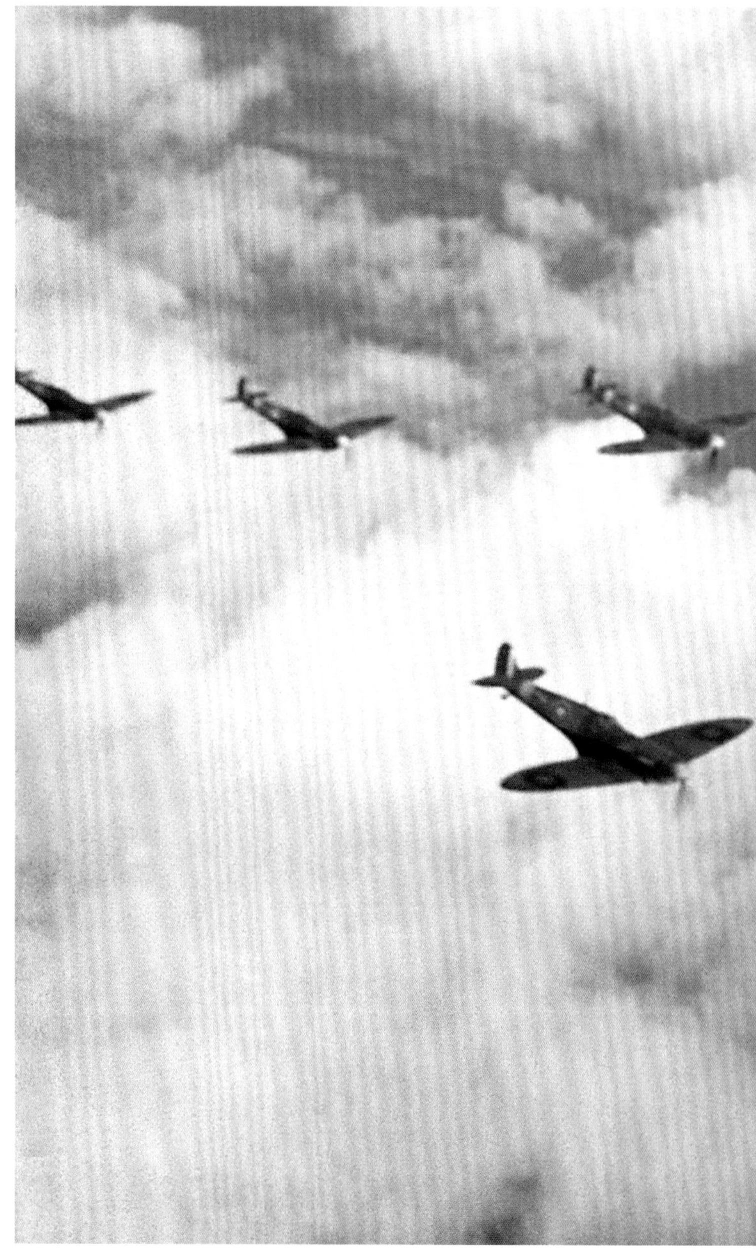

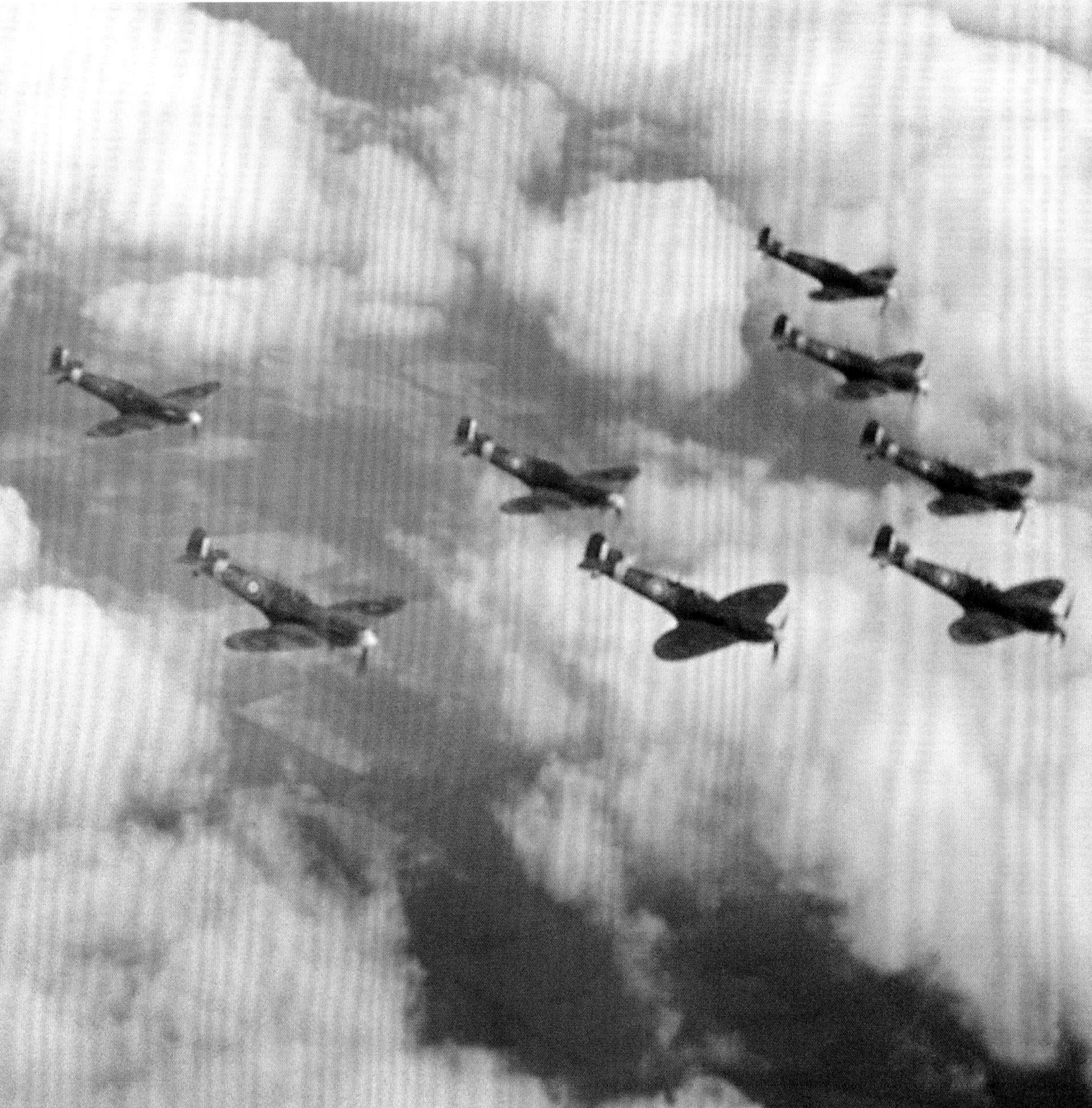

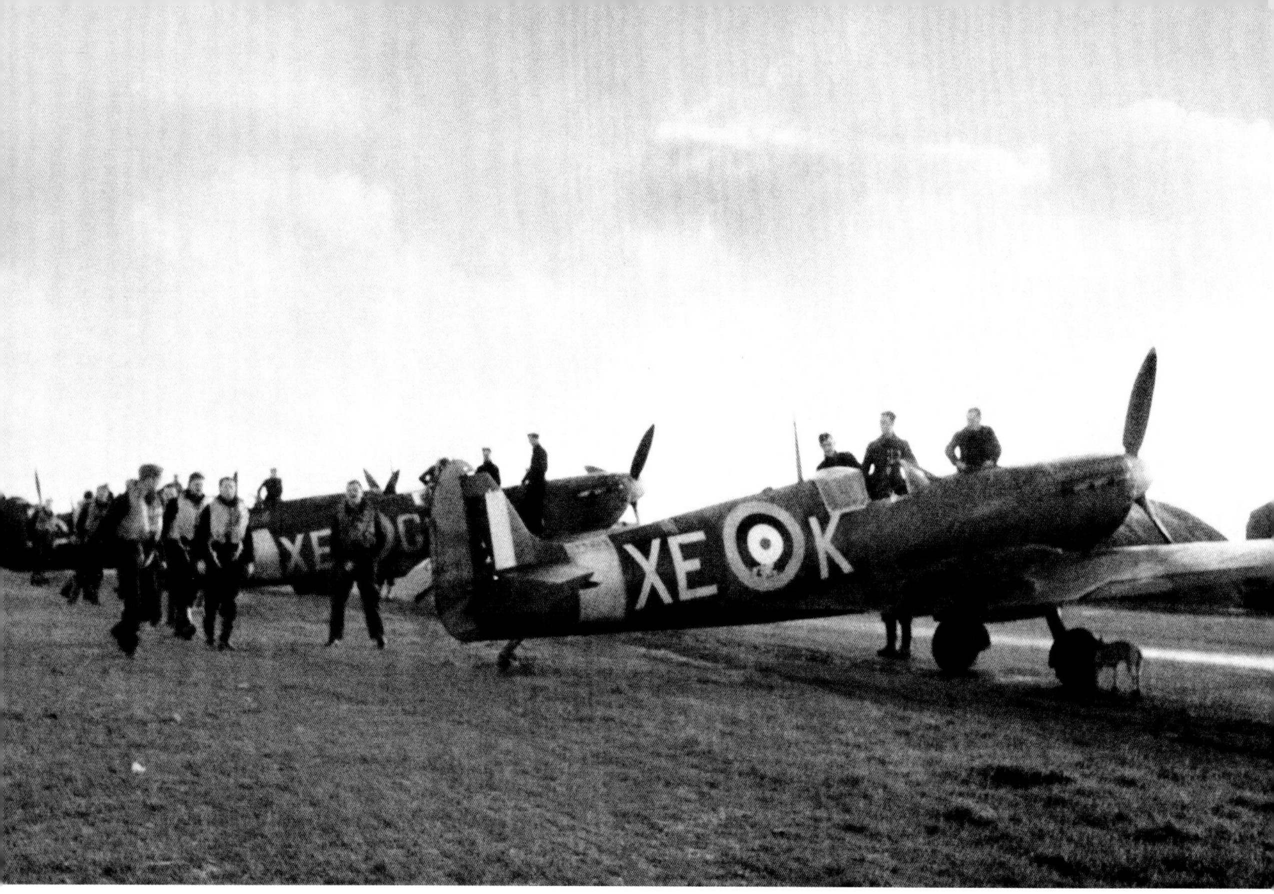
XE
XE K

Spitfire Mk IIA's ('XE-K', nearest) of 123 Squadron being prepared for a sortie at Castletown, Caithness, November 1941. While the Mk II was introduced in time to take part in the Battle of Britain, many were also used in offensive fighter 'sweeps' over occupied Europe from late 1940.

Spitfire Mk VB, R6923 'QJ-S', of 92 Squadron based at Biggin Hill, Kent, May 1941. The Mk V was developed as a 'stop-gap' while the more complex Mk III went into production, but proved itself capable enough to see the Mk III project cancelled altogether.

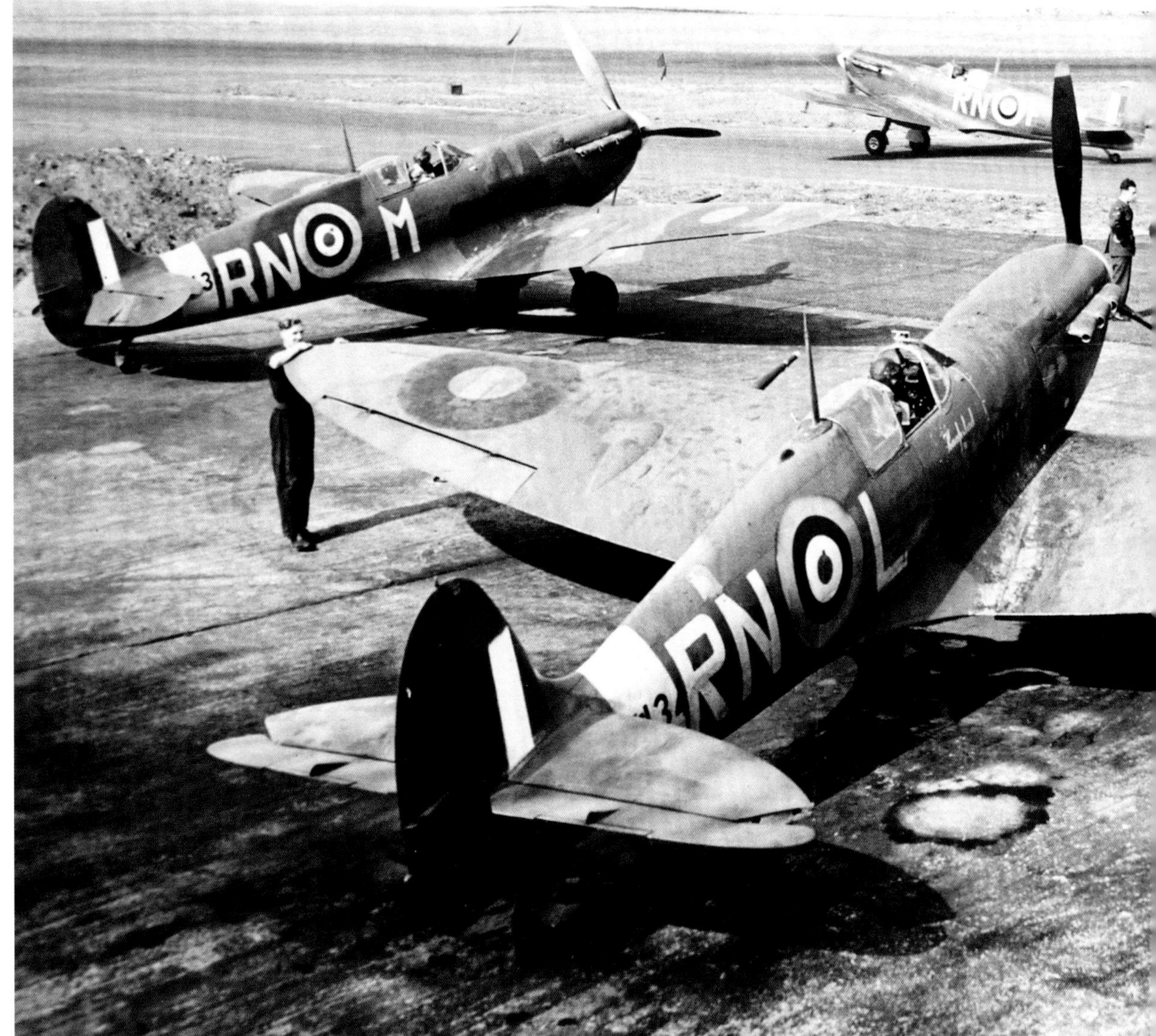
RN M
RN L
RN

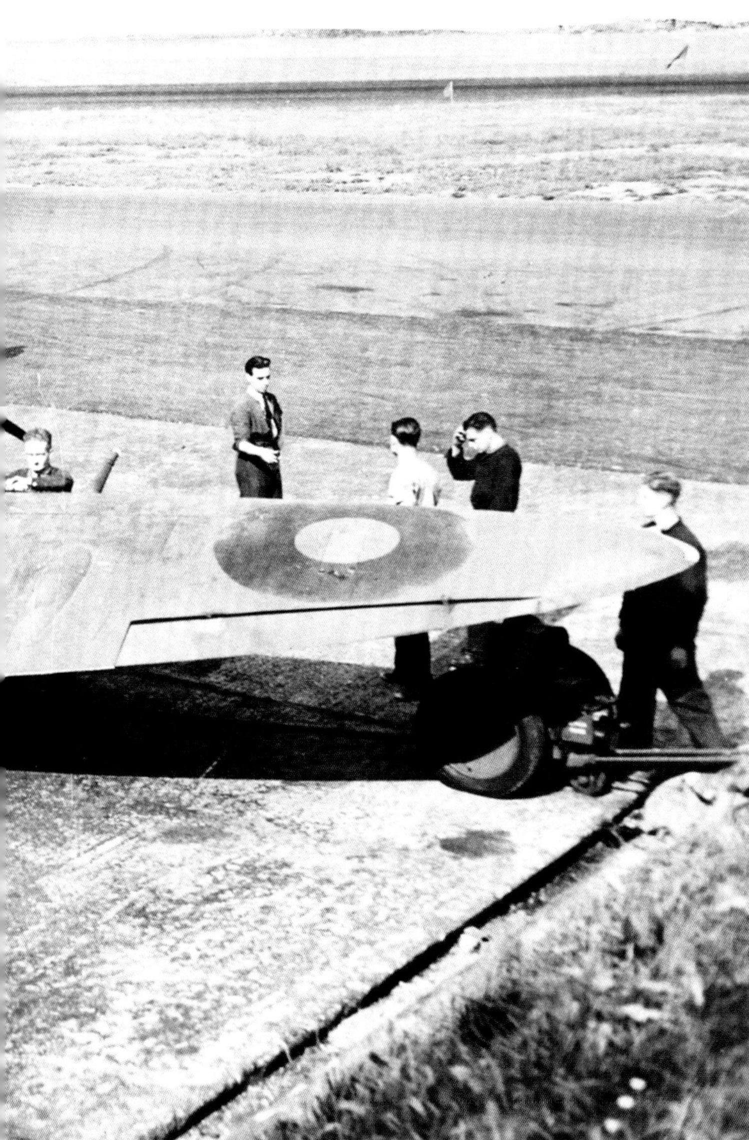

Three Spitfire Mk VB's of 72 Squadron about to take off on a fighter sweep, 1941. Utilising the same basic airframe design as the Mk I or II, the Mk V had a strengthened fuselage that could hold the more powerful Merlin 45 engine.

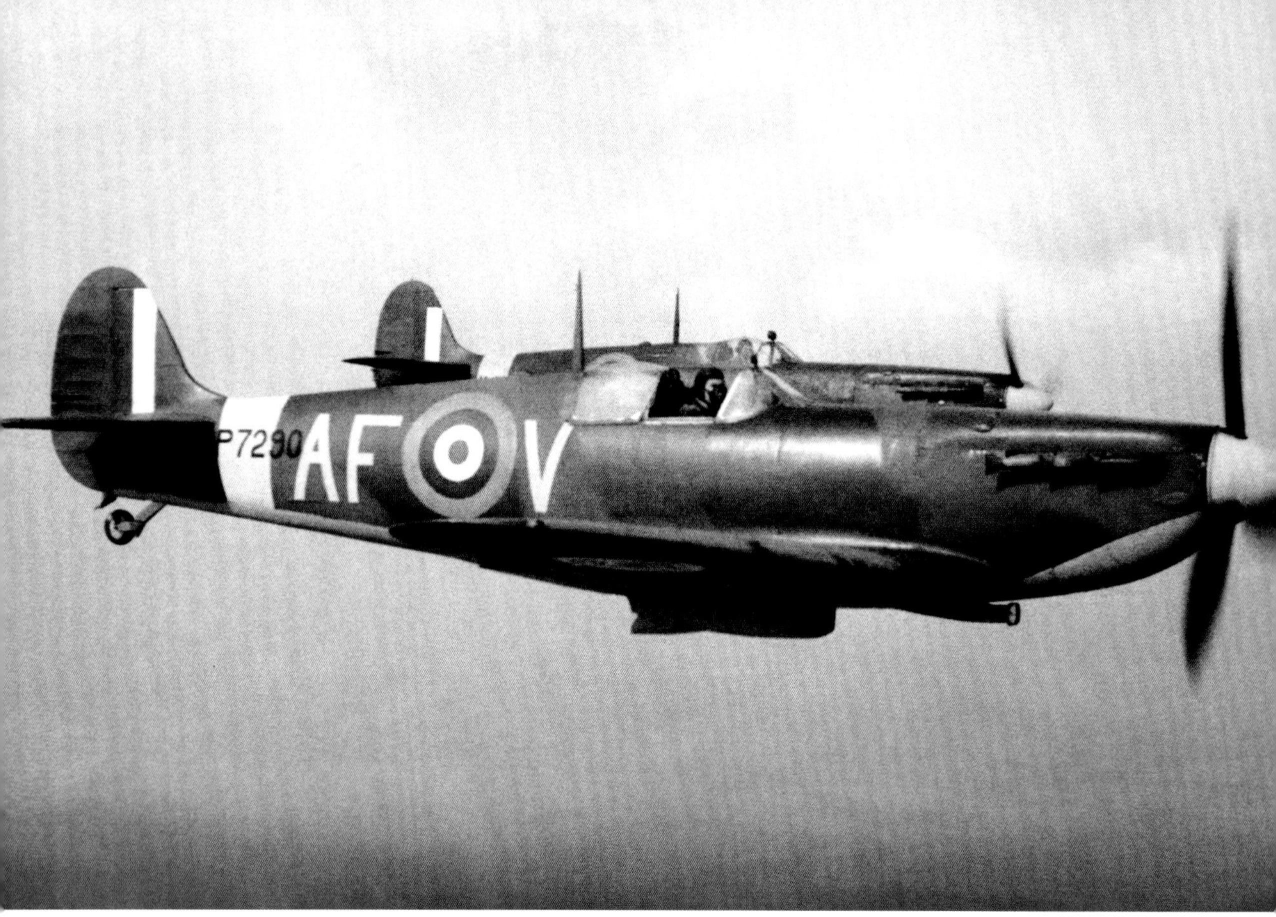
P7290
AF V

Spitfire Mk VA, P7290 'AF-V', of the Air Fighting Development Unit based at RAF Duxford, in flight with another aircraft of the unit, April 1942. P7290 was originally a Mk IIA, but like many Mk II's and I's was converted to Mk V standard.

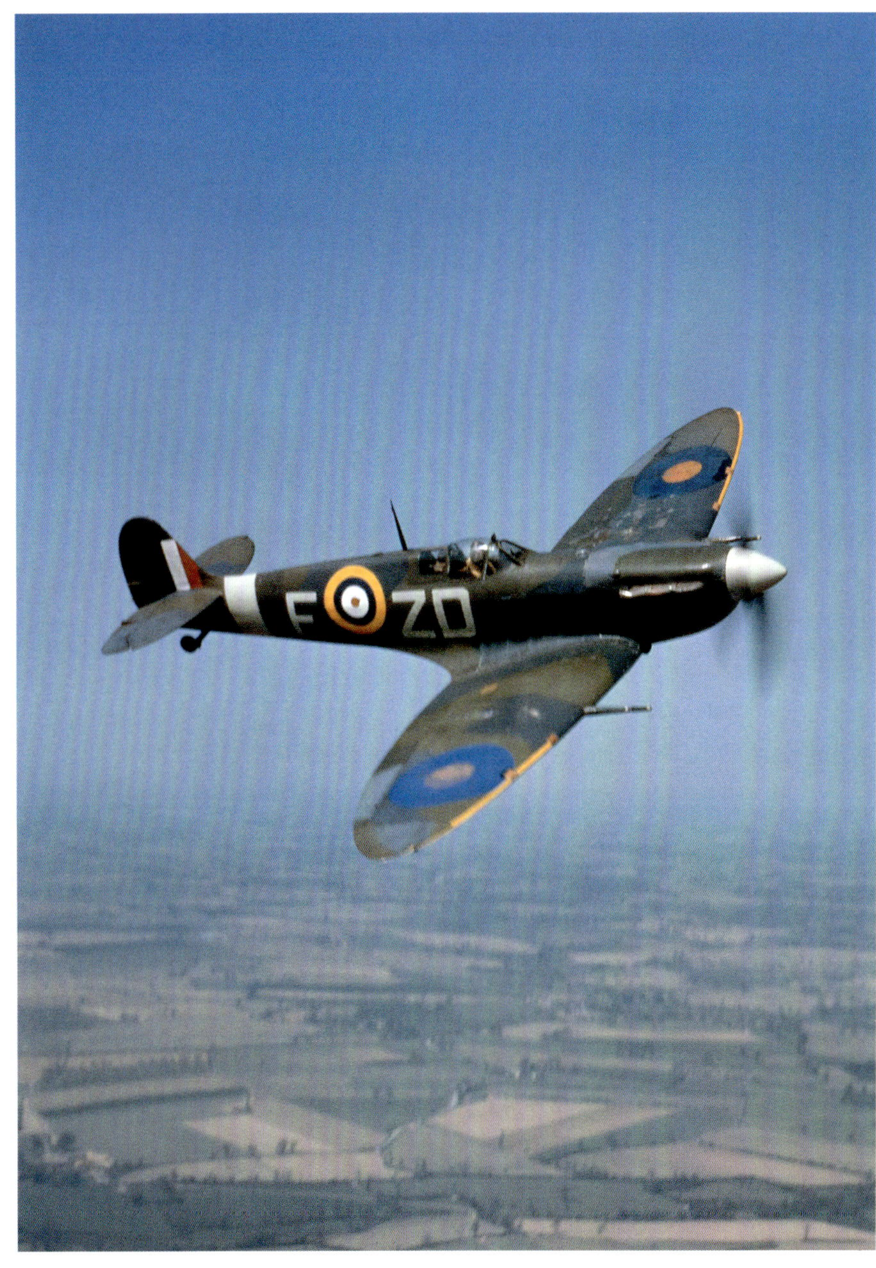

Spitfire Mk VB, AD233 'ZD-F' of 222 Squadron, based at North Weald, Essex, in flight, May 1942. The majority of Mk V's were built with 'B' type wings, which were fitted with two 20mm Hispano cannons, seen projecting from the wings, in addition to four machine guns.

Spitfire Mk VB's (ES187 'C' and ES191 'T', nearest) of 154 Squadron being brought to readiness by ground crew at Tingley, Algeria, March 1943. The Mk V became the most produced Spitfire mark, making up nearly a third of the total number of Spitfires built.

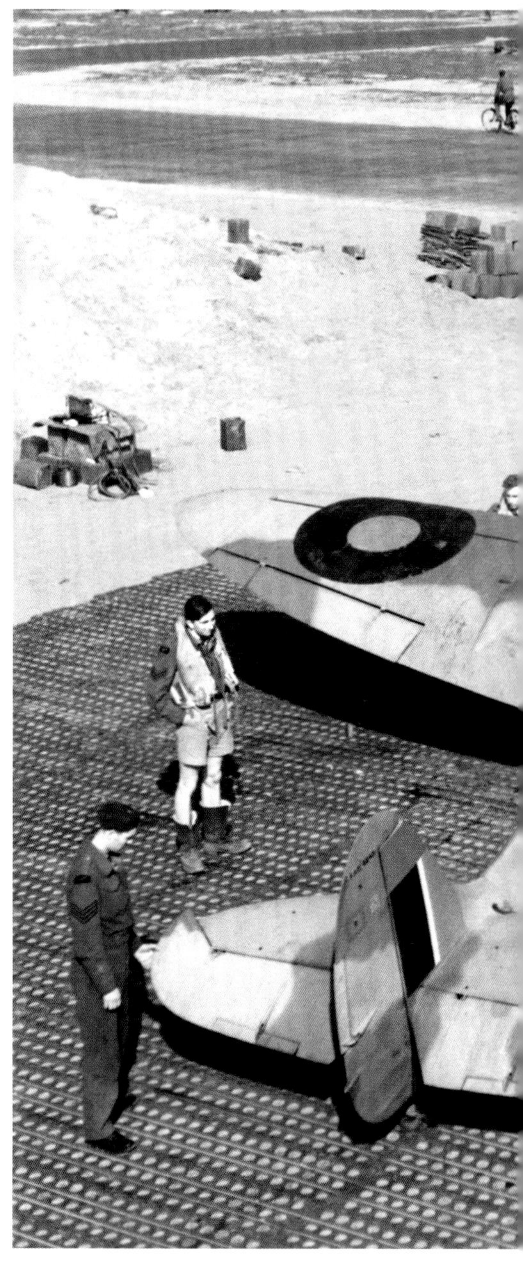

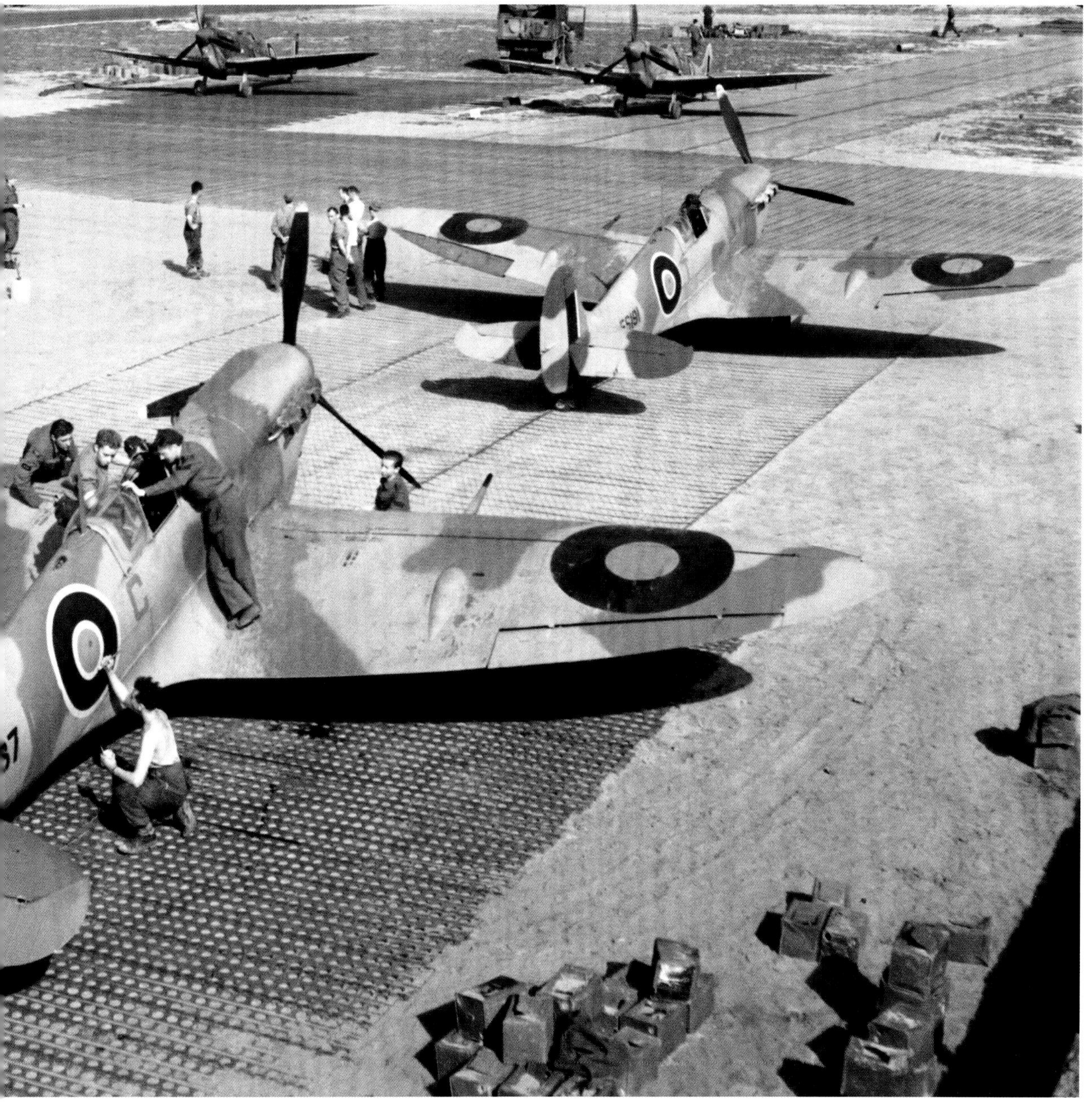

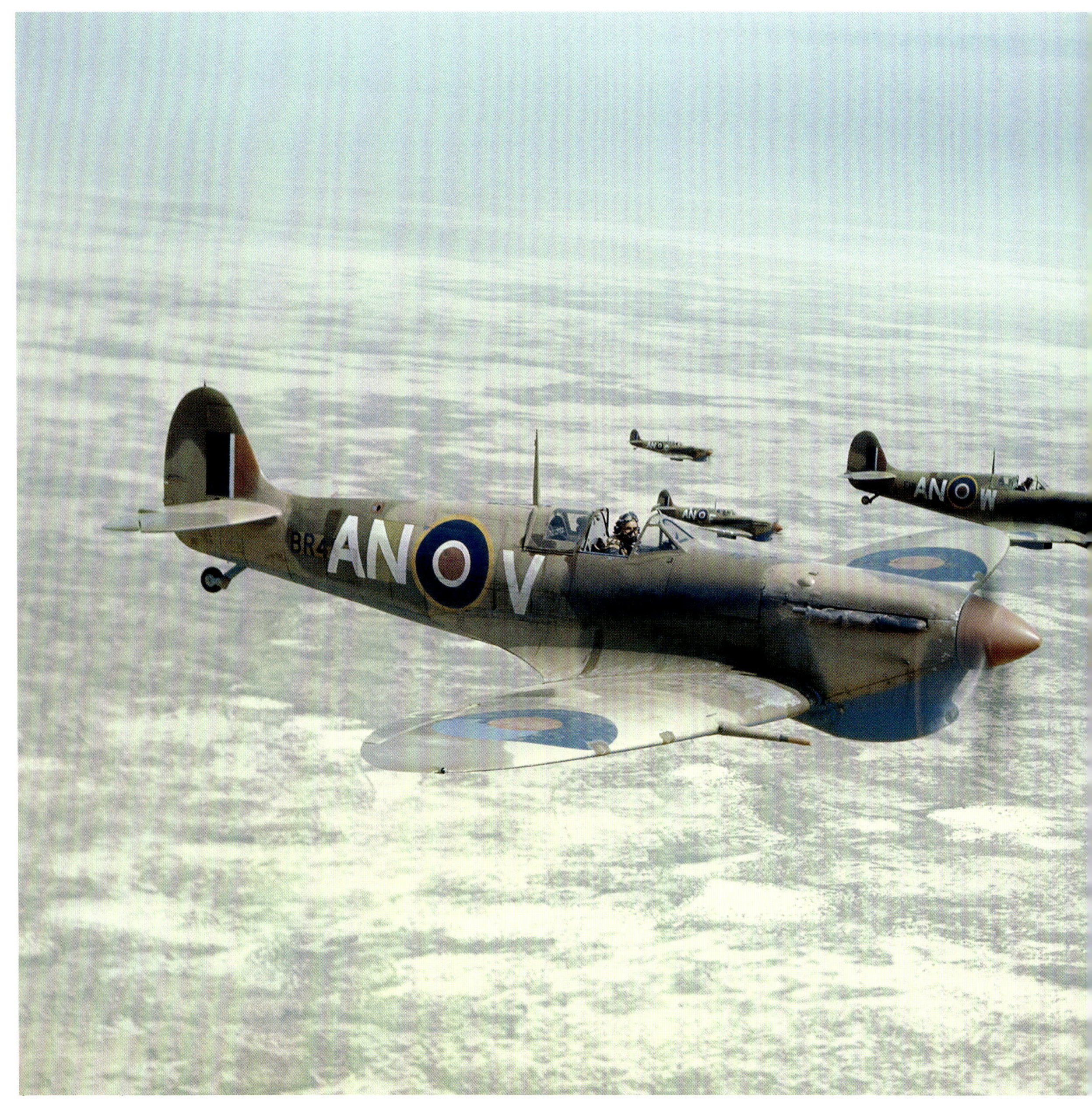
AN V
AN W

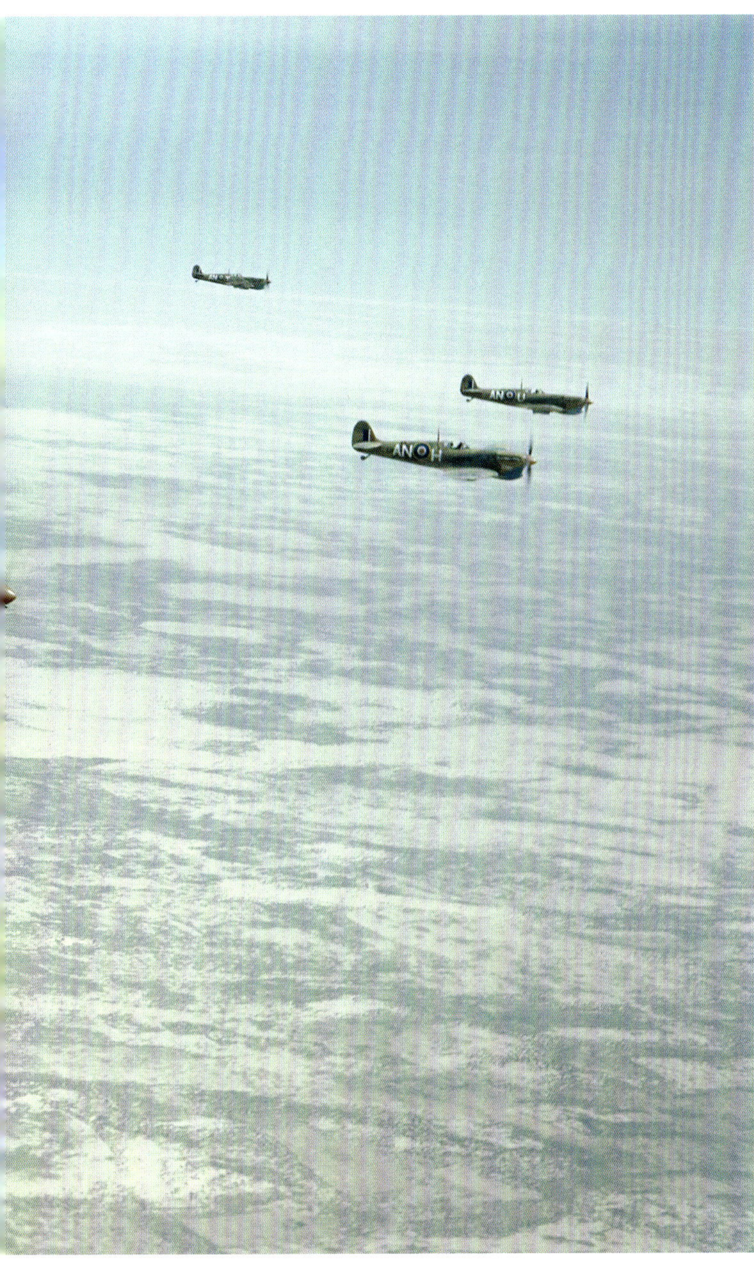

Spitfire Mk VB's (Tropical) of 417 Squadron, Royal Canadian Air Force (RCAF), flying in loose formation over the Tunisian desert, April 1943. The tropical variant featured a special air filter under the nose, which prevented sand and dust from damaging the engine.

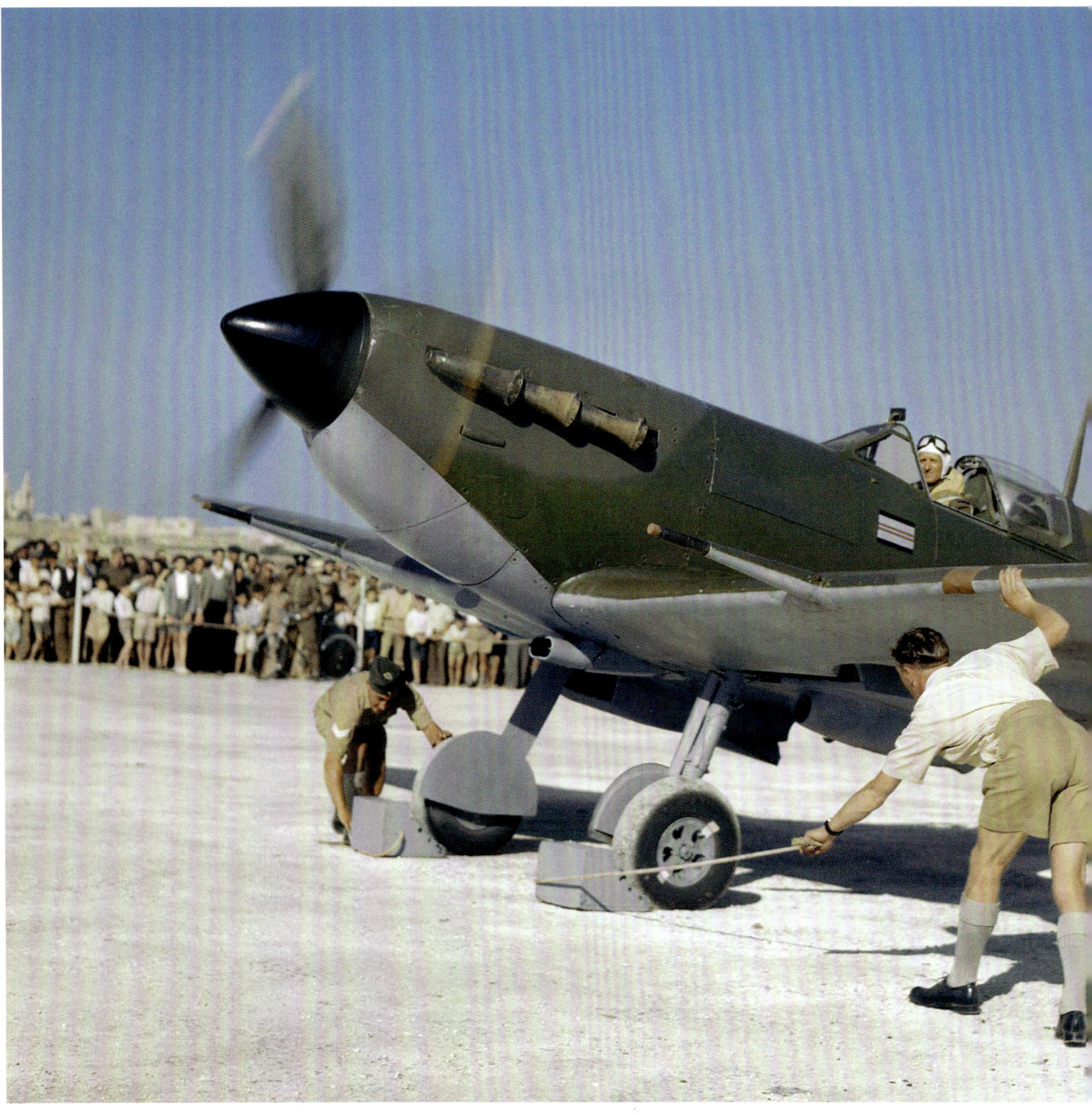

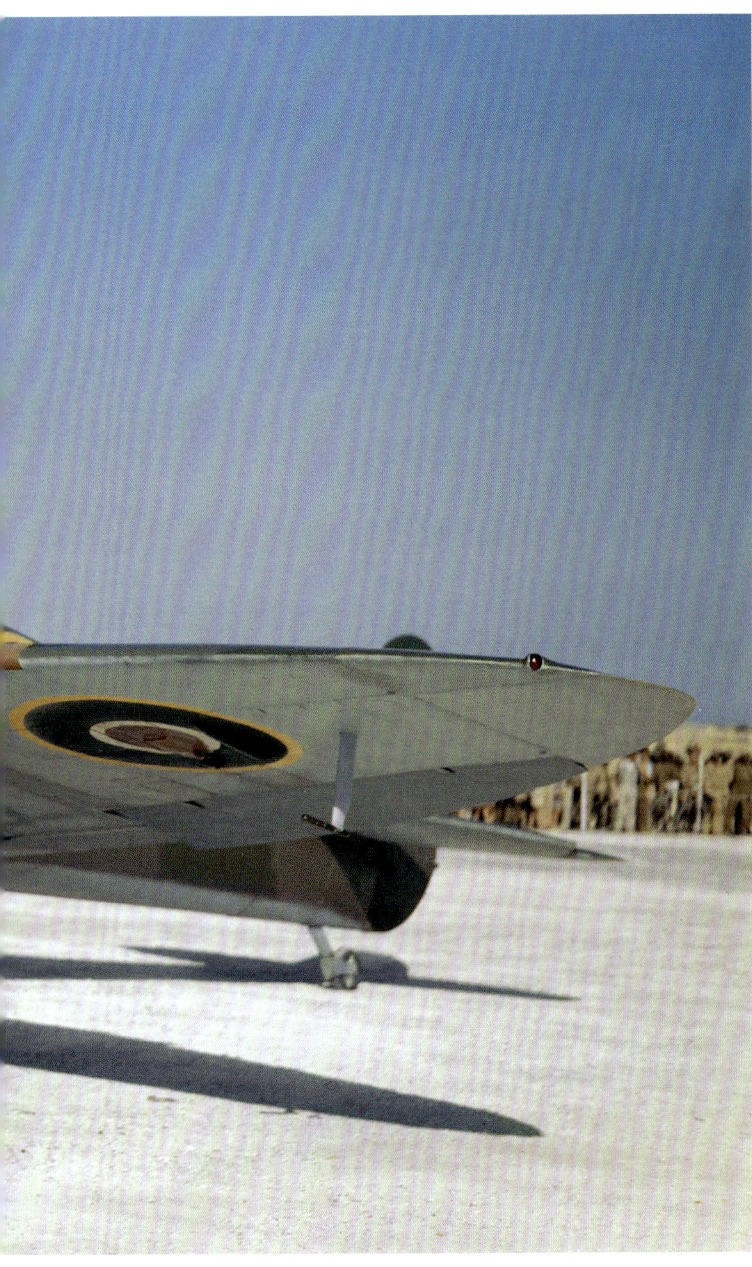

Air Officer Commanding (AOC) Malta, Air Vice Marshal Keith Park in his personal Spitfire Mk VB at Safi, Malta, May 1943. Spitfire Mk V's played a key role in the air defence of Malta, which Park oversaw from July 1942.

A pilot of 152 Squadron climbs into the cockpit of Spitfire Mk VC (Tropical), JG871 'L-E', at Souk-el-Khemis, Tunisia, April 1943. Built with the 'C' type wing, Mk VC's were shipped in large numbers to Australia, Burma and the Mediterranean.

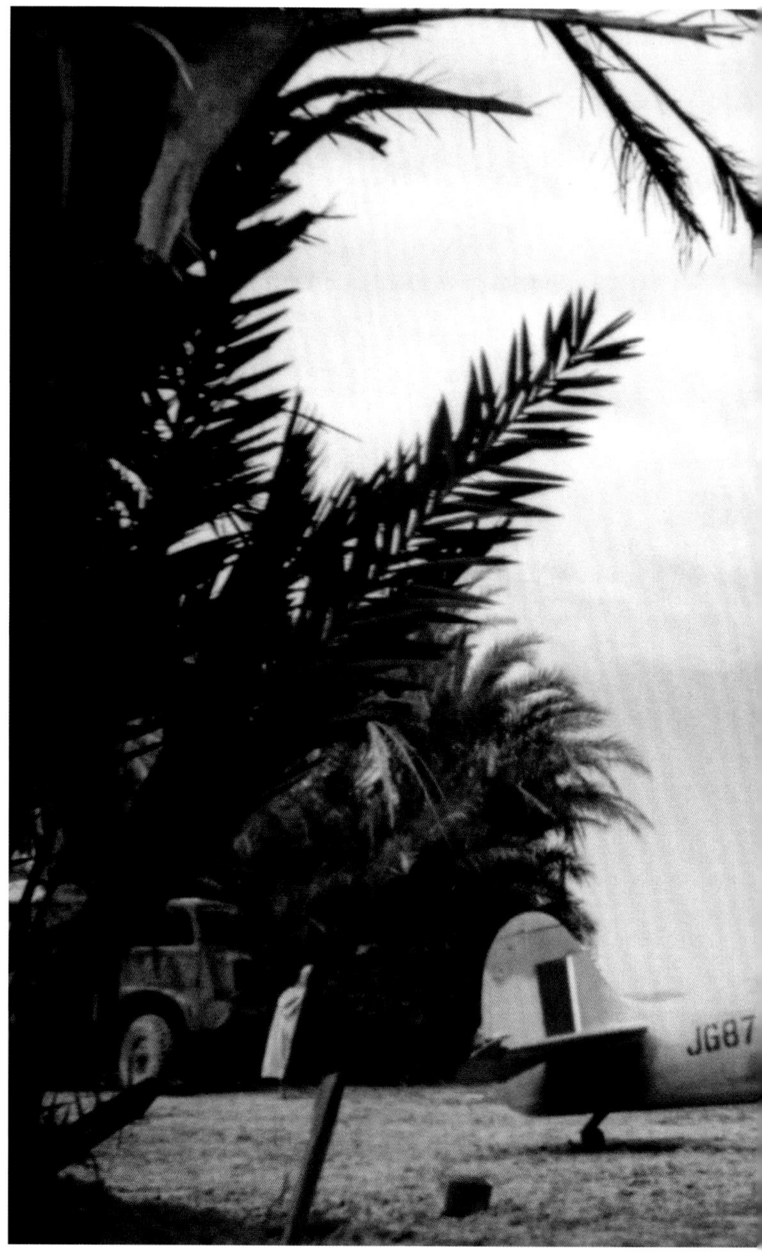

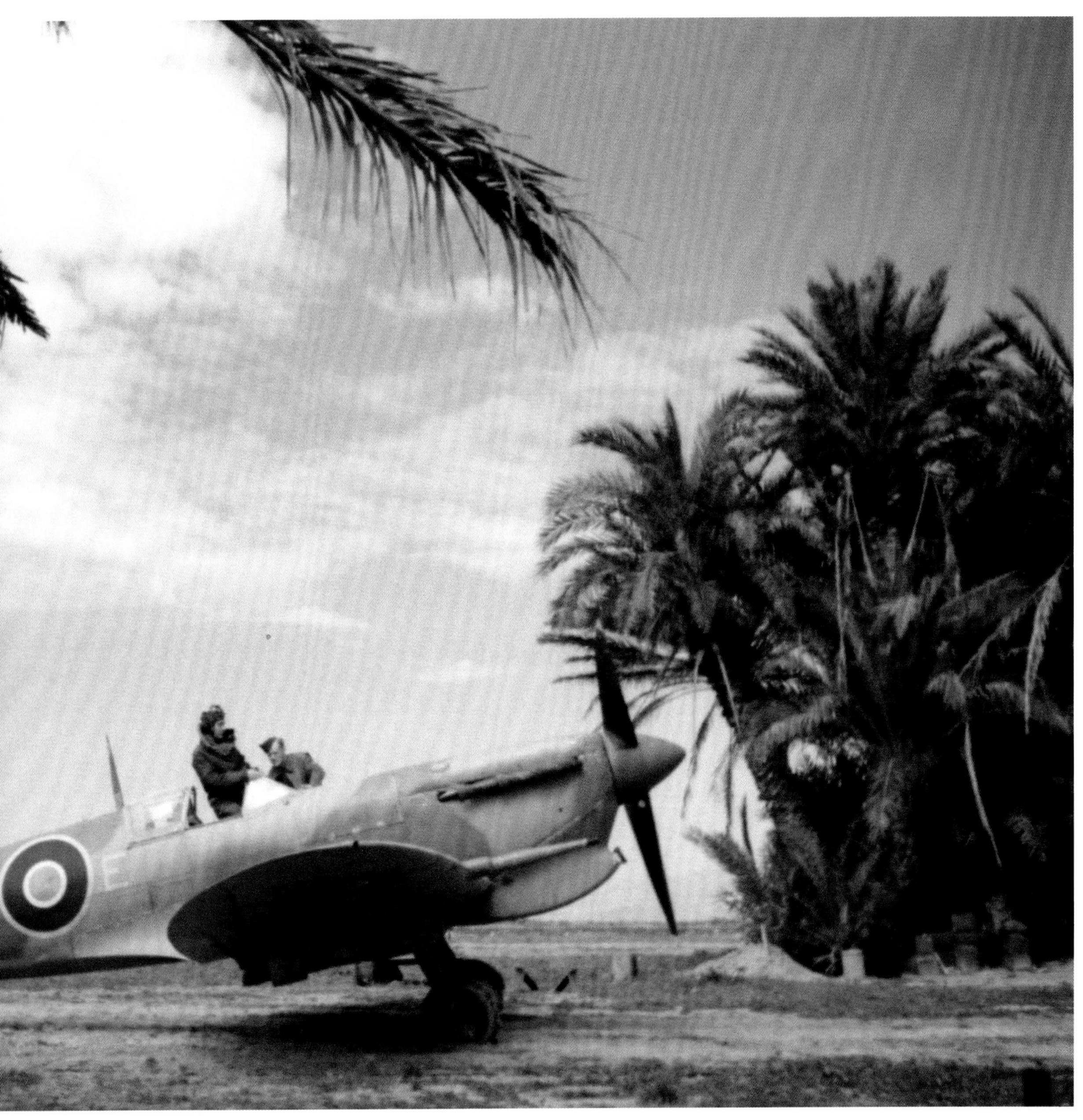

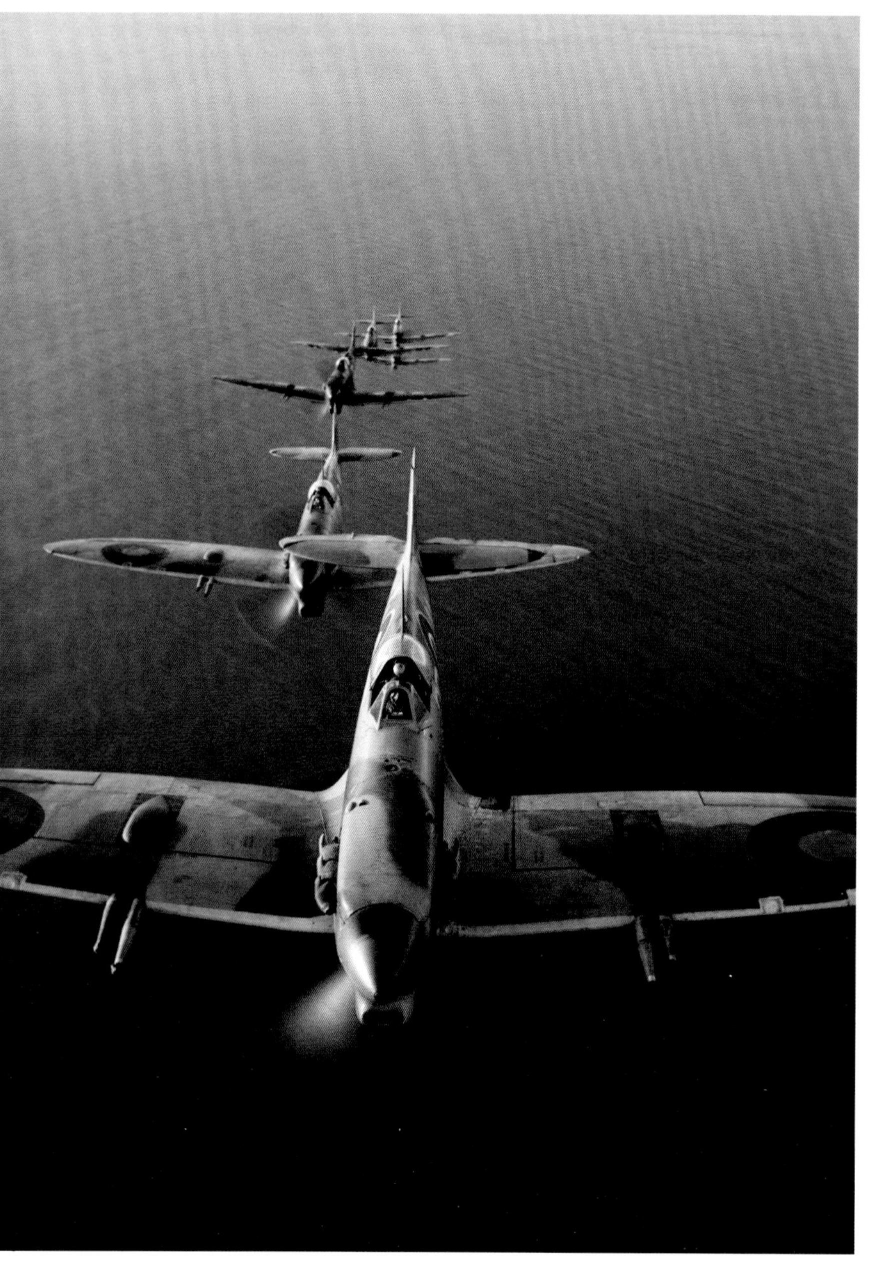

Spitfire Mk VC's (Tropical) of 2 Squadron South African Air Force (SAAF) based at Palata, Italy, flying over the Adriatic Sea while on a bombing mission, November 1943. 'C' type wings could be fitted with four 20mm cannon, and were the first type that could carry bombs.

Spitfire Mk VI, BR579 'ON-H', of 124 Squadron, at North Weald, Essex, November 1943. The Mk VI was designed in response to the development of high altitude German bombers. Capable of flying as high as 40,000 feet, it featured extended wingtips, a four-bladed propeller and a pressurised cockpit.

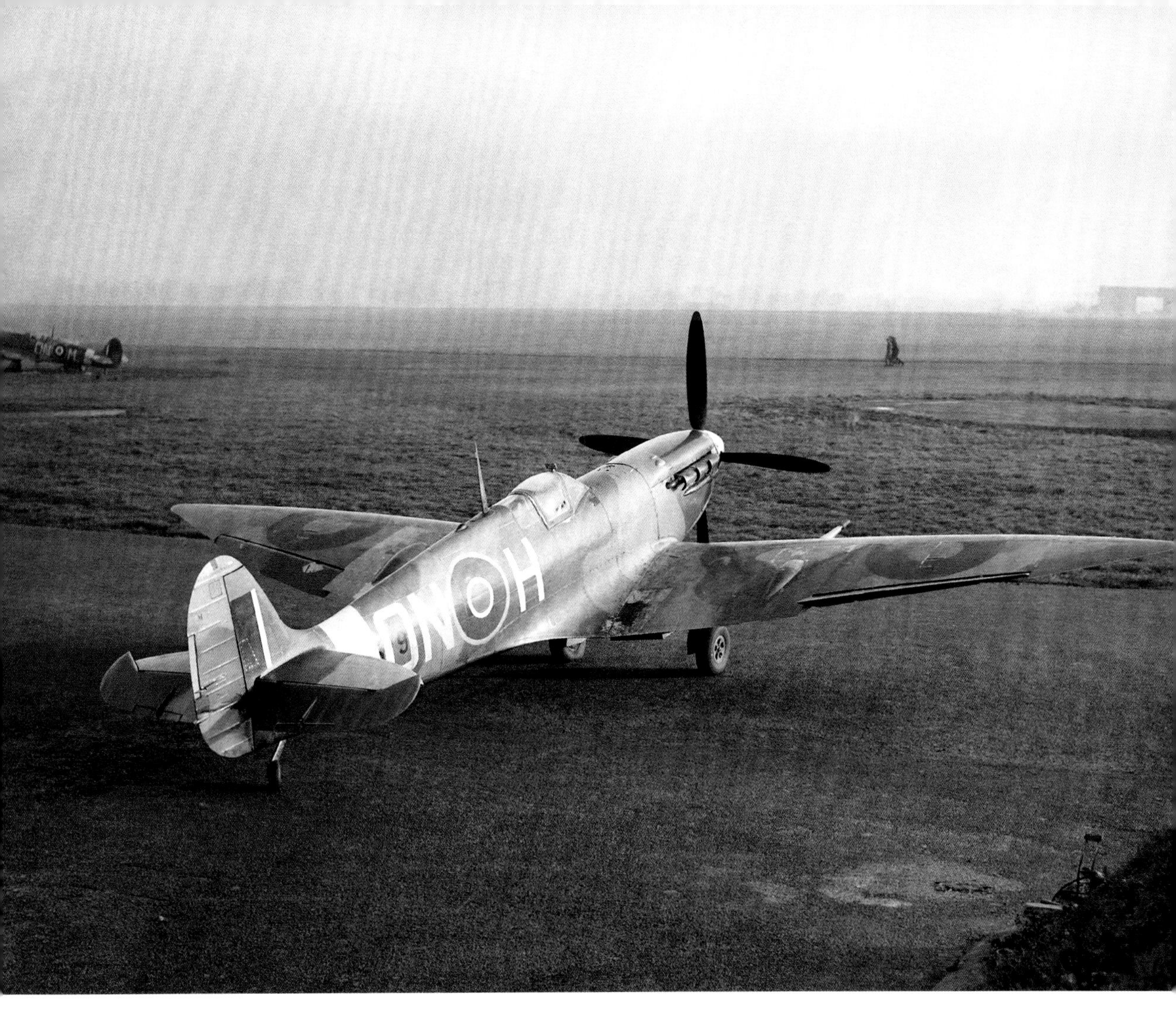
DN H

Spitfire Mk IX's of 611 Squadron flying in formation, December 1942. Due to the slow development of the Mk VIII, the Mk IX was introduced as a temporary answer to the Luftwaffe's Focke-Wulf Fw 190, which easily outclassed the Mk V in combat.

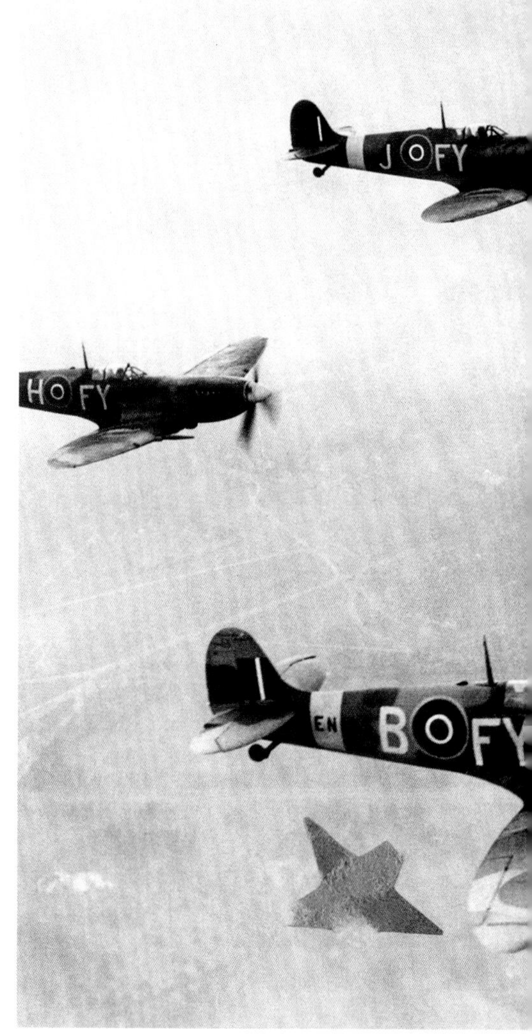

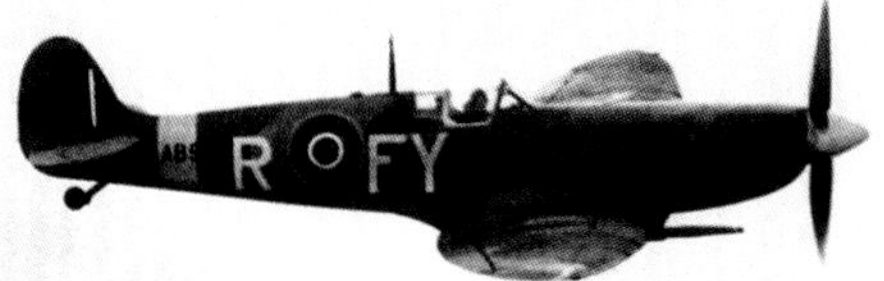
R
FY

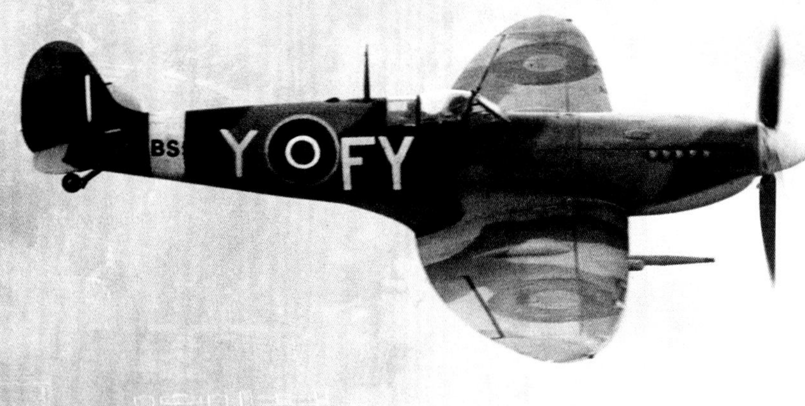
Y
FY

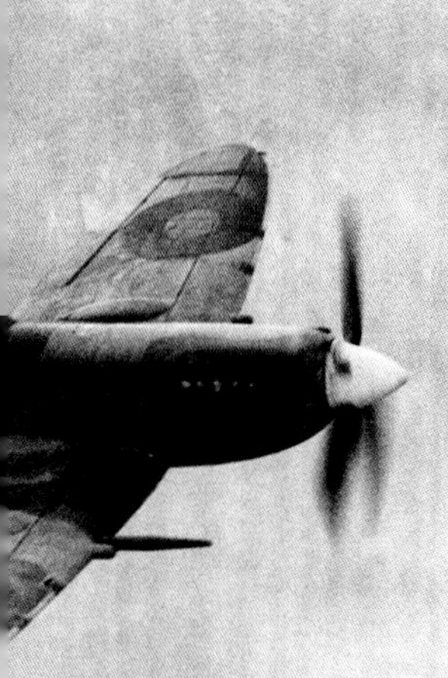

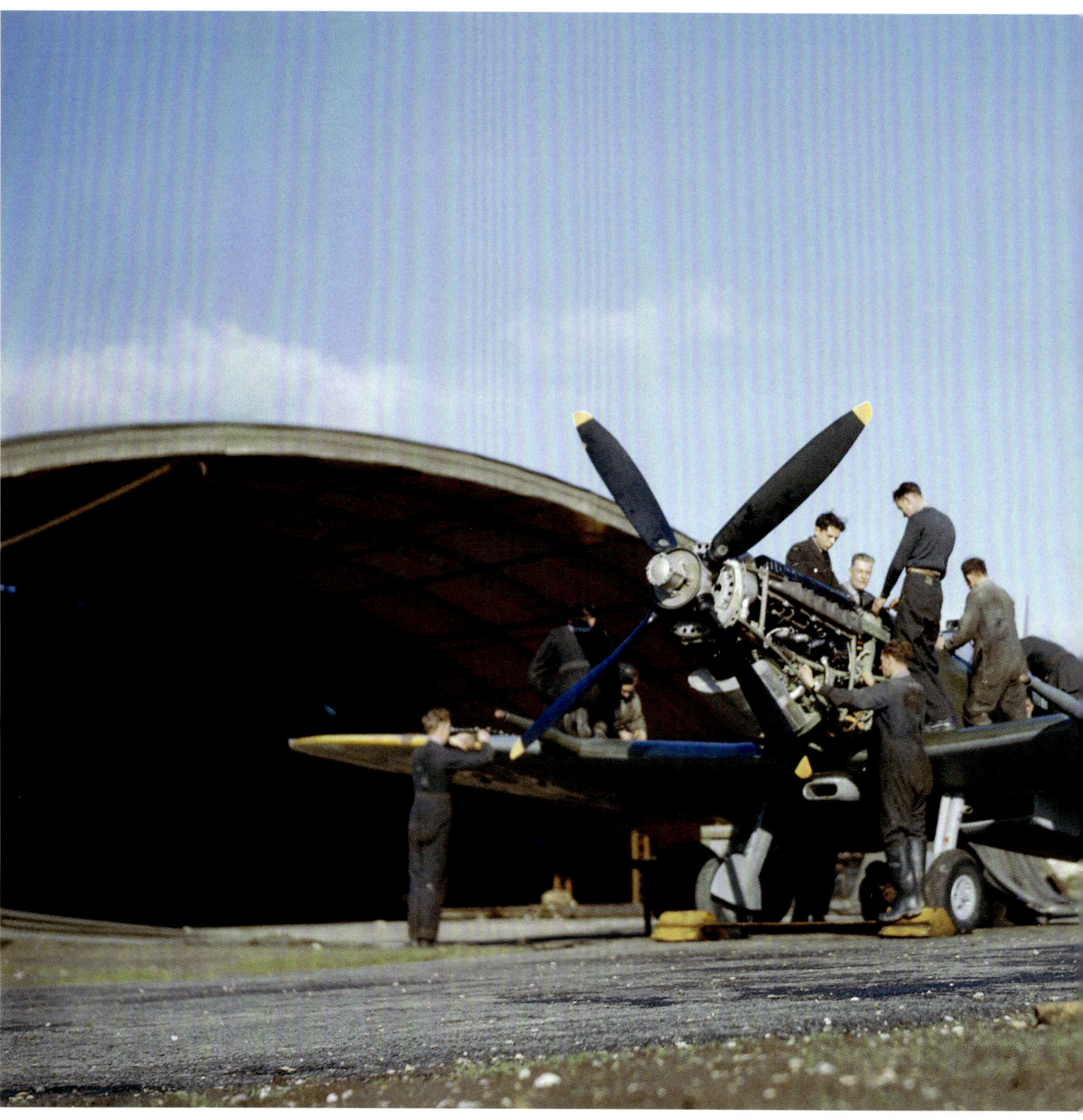

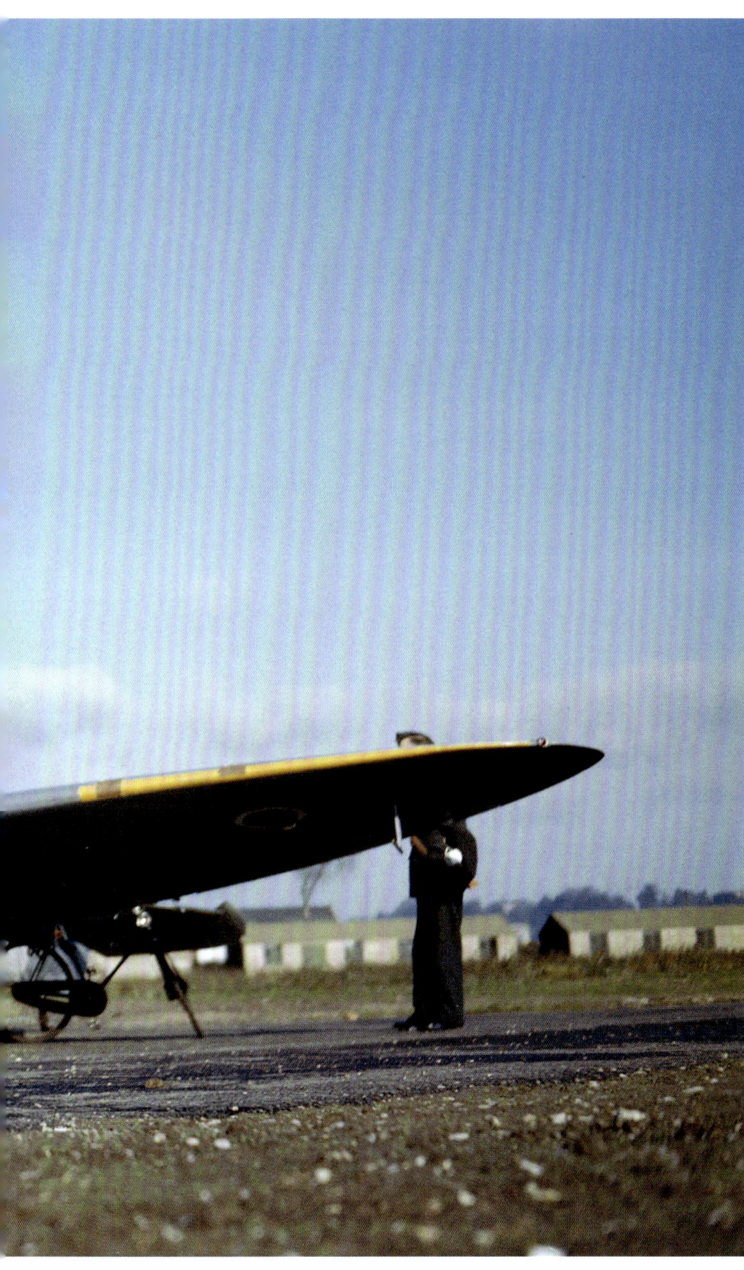

A Spitfire Mk IX of 64 Squadron undergoing an engine overhaul at Fairlop, Essex, November 1942. Just as the Mk V utilised Mk I and II airframes, early Mk IX Spitfires were built using Mk V airframes, but fitted with the much more powerful two-stage supercharged Merlin 61 engine driving a four-bladed propeller.

An armourer adjusts one of the machine guns on Spitfire Mk IX, BS538 'NL-B', of 341 (Free French) Squadron, at Biggin Hill, Kent, May 1943. The Mk IX restored parity with the Focke-Wulf Fw 190, allowing the RAF to regain the initiative over occupied Europe.

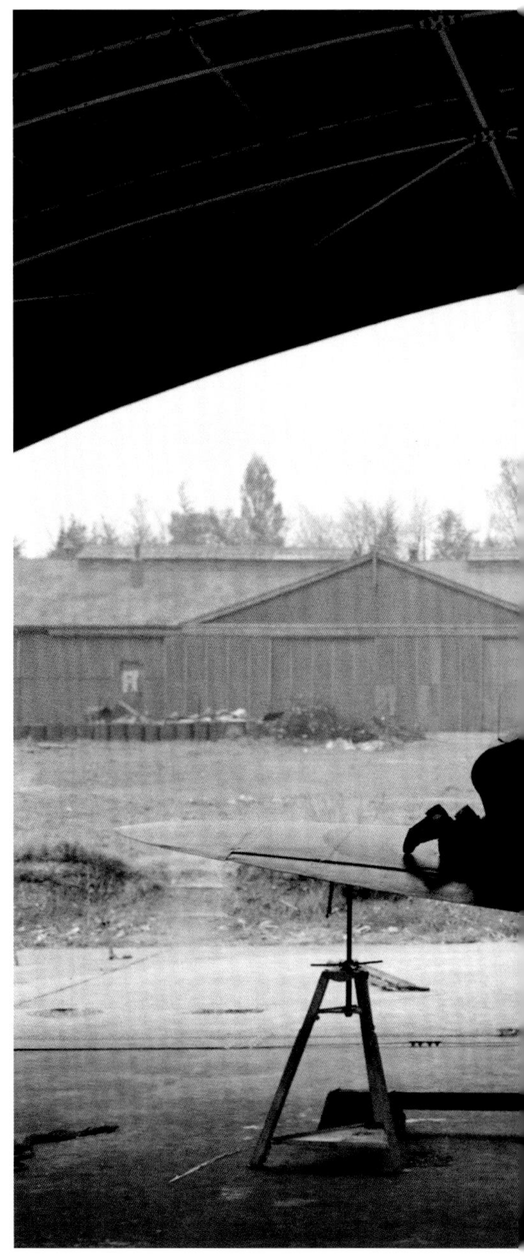

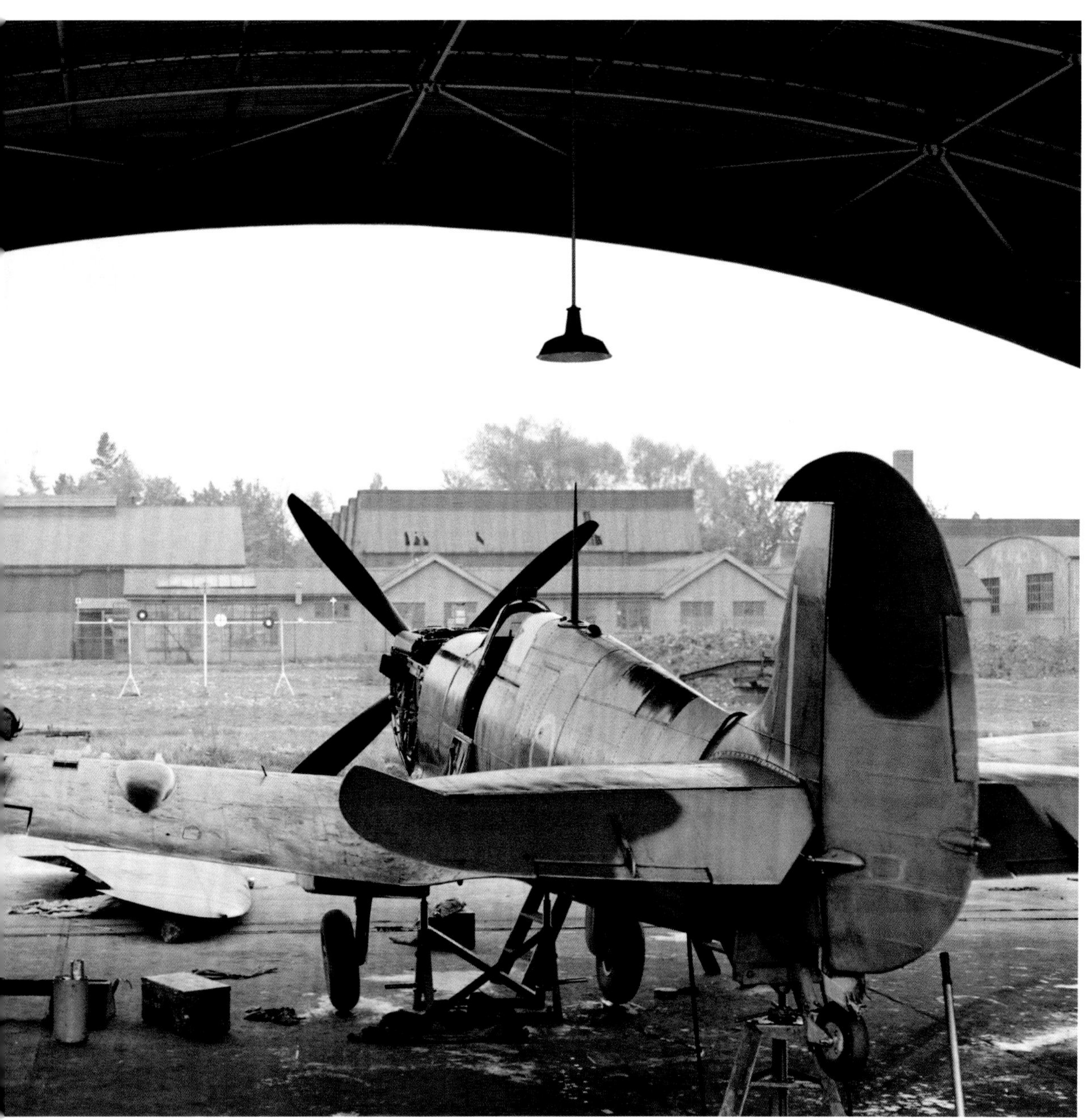

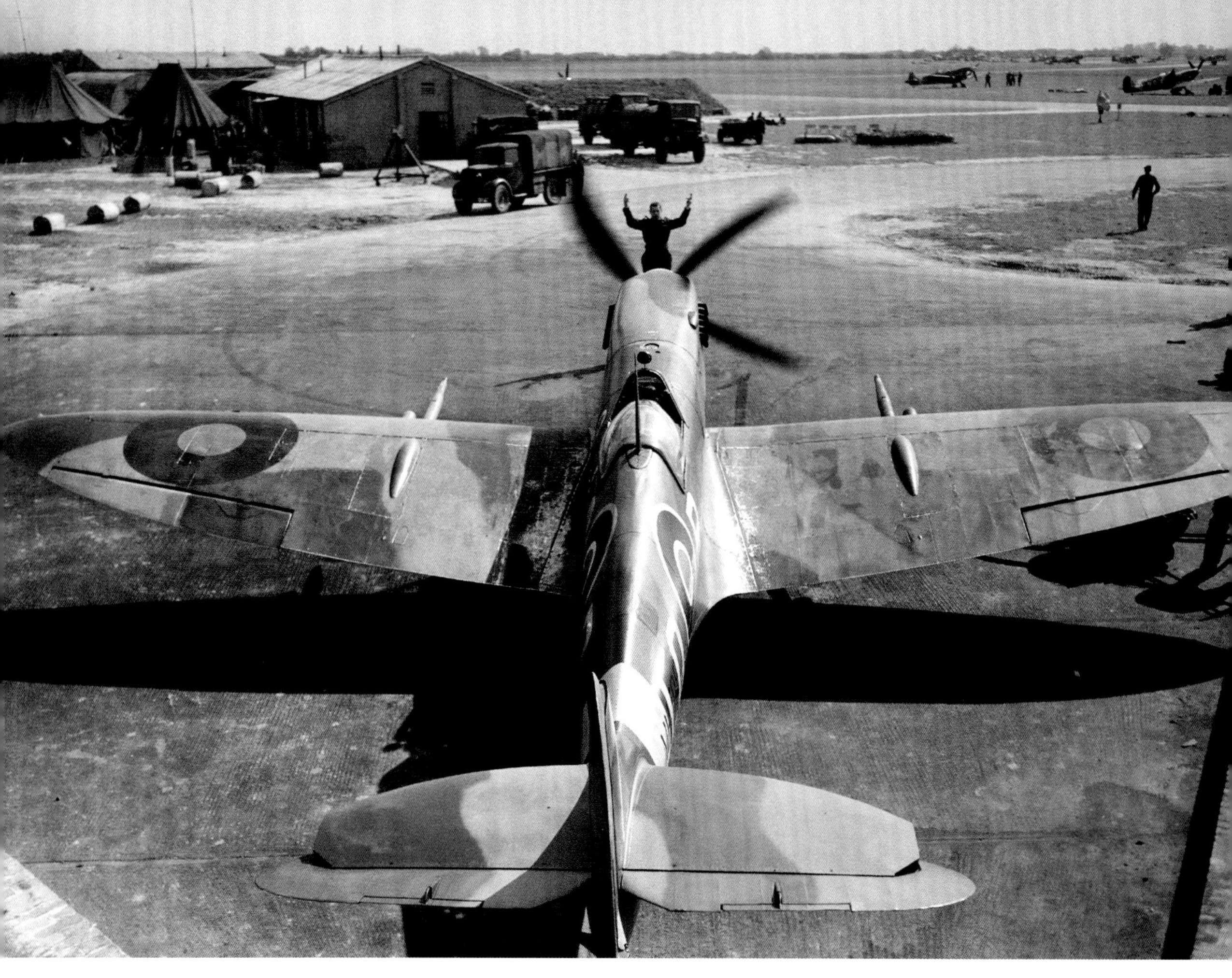

Spitfire LF Mk IX 'LO-P' of 602 Squadron is guided out from its dispersal at Ford, Sussex, for a fighter sweep over occupied Europe, April 1944. The Mk IX was such a success that it became the second most produced Spitfire mark, with nearly 6,000 built.

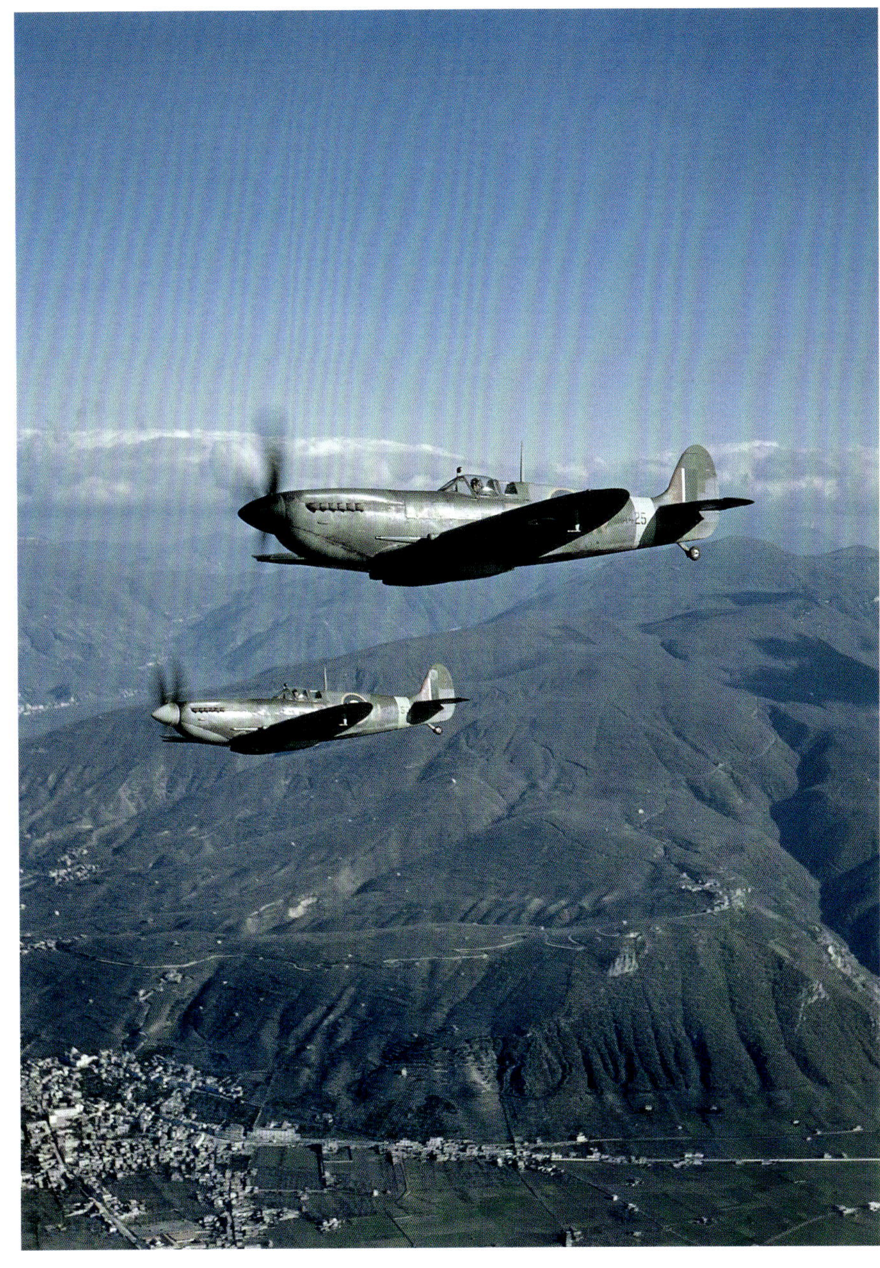

Two Spitfire Mk IX's of 241 Squadron, MA425 'RZ-R' and MH635 'RZ-U', flying over mountainous country south of Rome, January 1944. The two-stage supercharged Merlin engine dramatically improved the performance of the Spitfire, giving it a nearly 40mph increase in speed and the ability to fly at much higher altitudes.

Spitfire LF Mk IX's of 66 Squadron based at Bognor Regis, Sussex, flying to Normandy to provide a cover patrol over the beachhead, June 1944. The Mk IX made up the bulk of the RAF's fighters on D-Day, and played a key role in winning air superiority over Normandy.

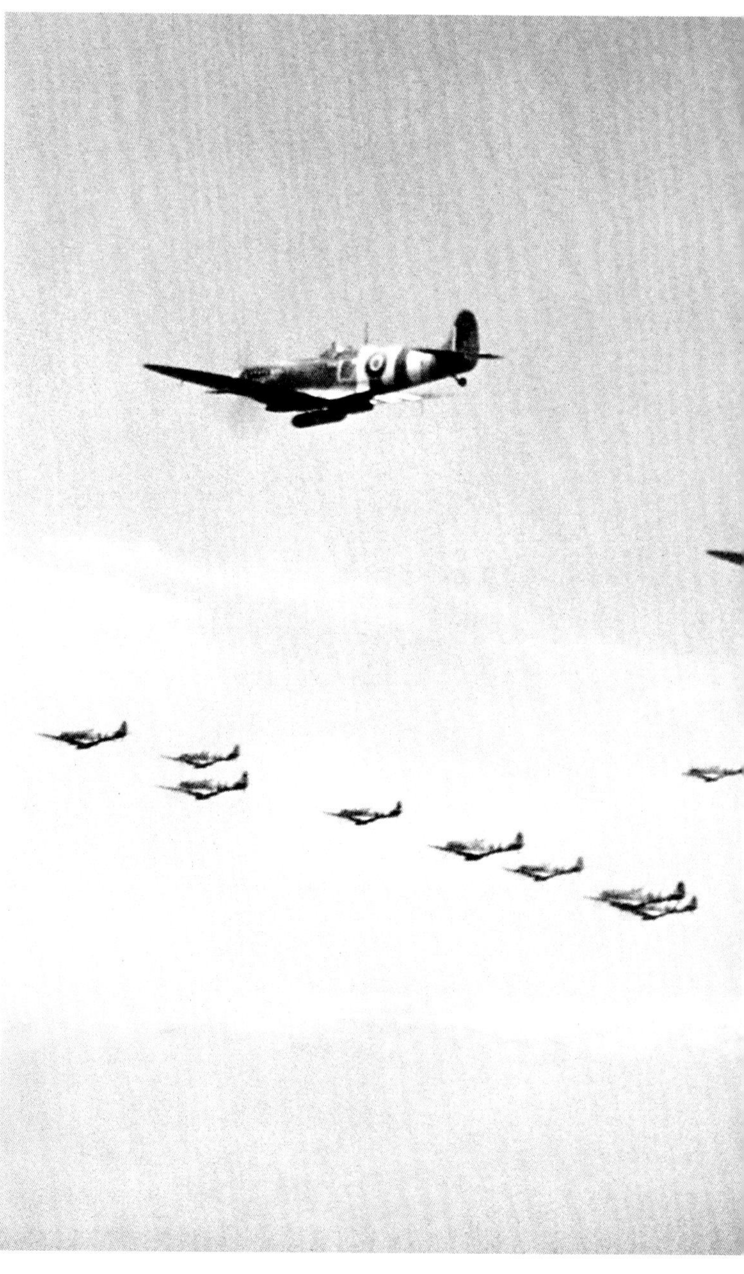

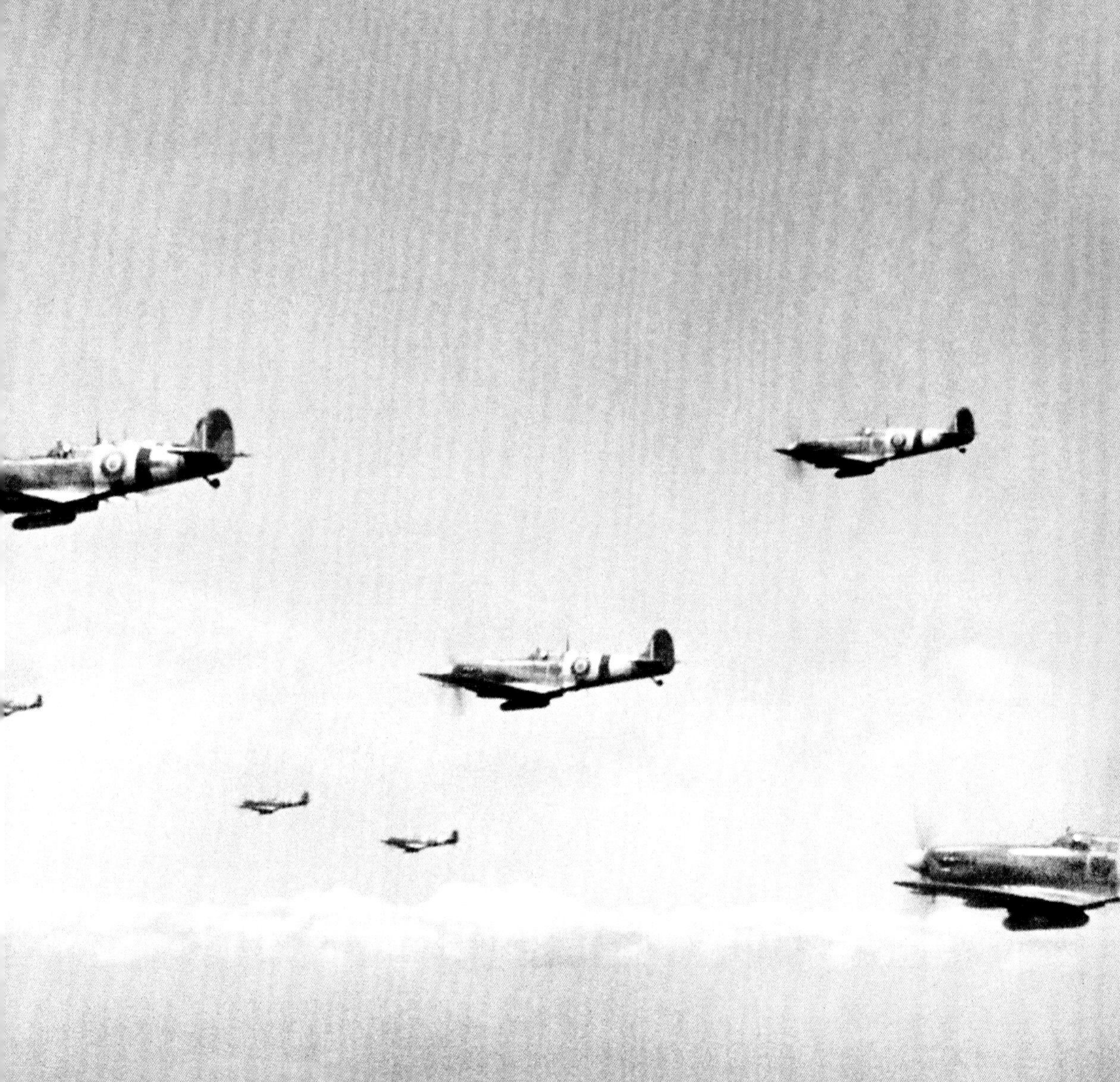

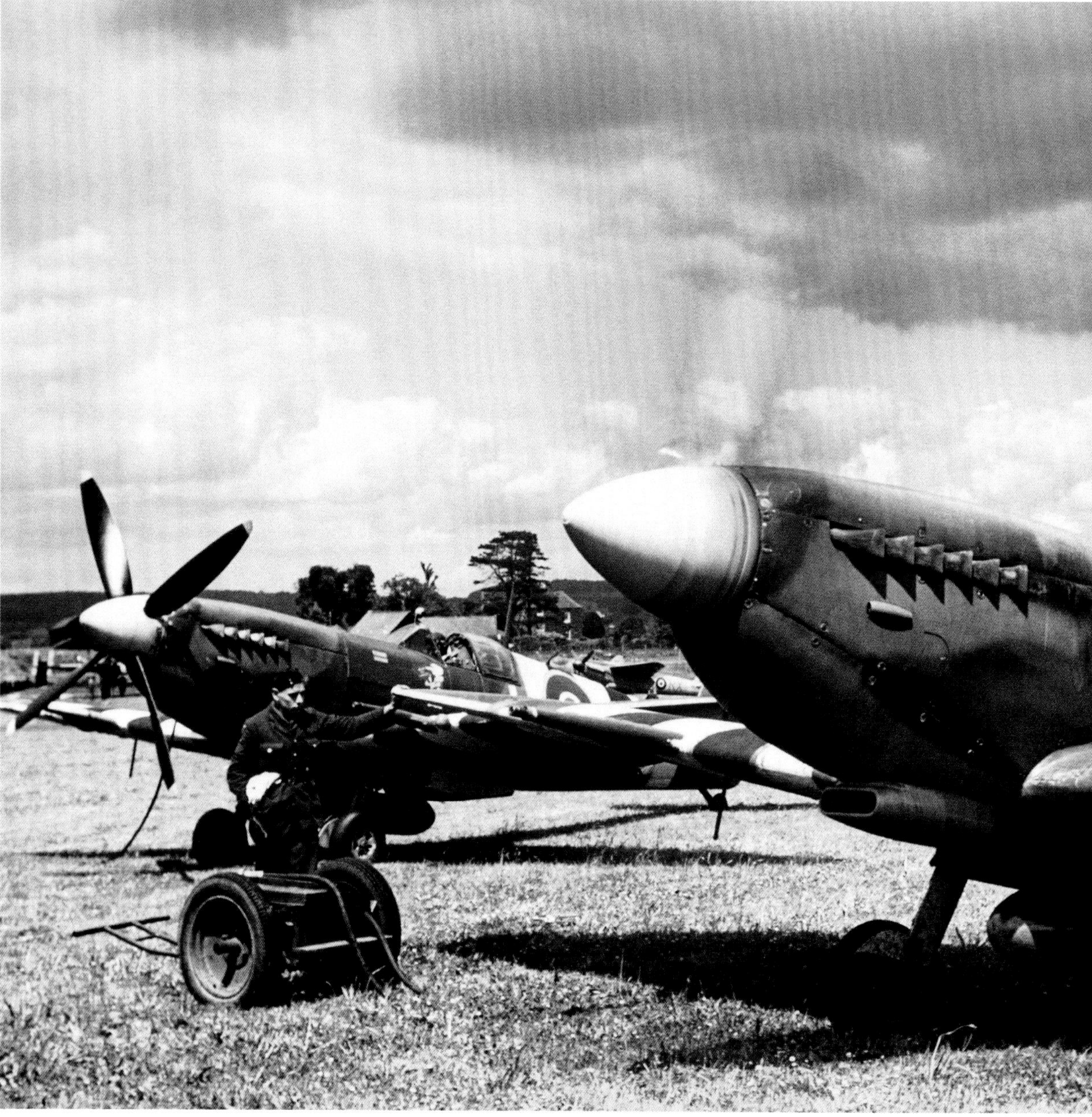

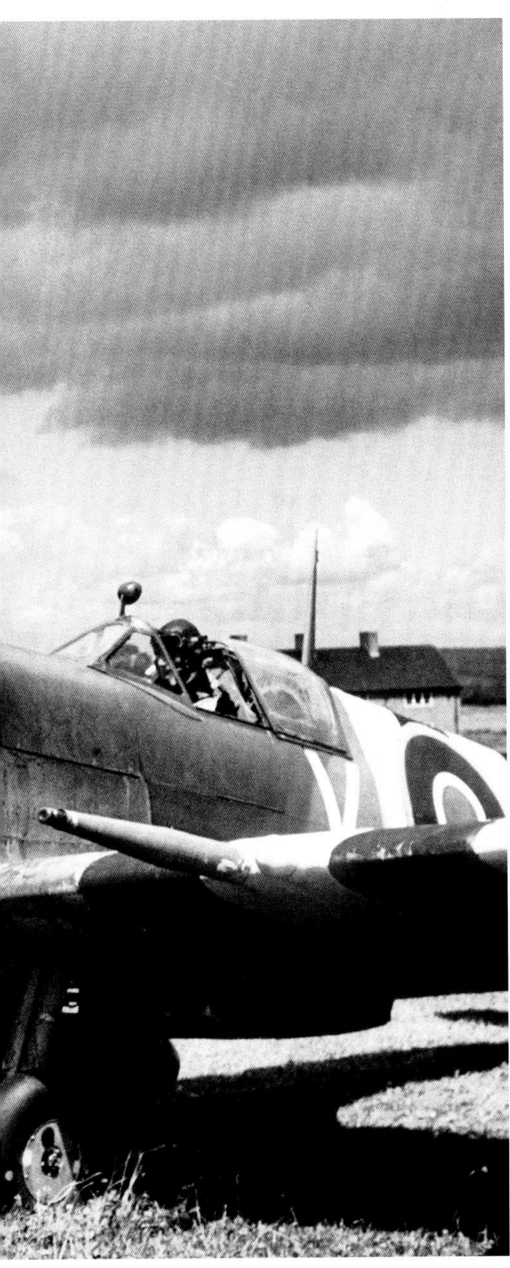

Spitfire LF Mk IX's of 453 Squadron, Royal Australian Air Force (RAAF), carrying long-range fuel tanks, start up at Ford, Sussex, for operations over Normandy, June 1944. Drop tanks extended the Spitfire's range, enabling it to mount longer standing patrols as well as perform bomber escort duties.

Spitfire Mk IXE's of 412 Squadron, RCAF, await the start-up signal, Volkel, Holland, October 1944. First introduced on the Mk IX, the 'E' type wing enabled the aircraft to carry two 250lb wing-mounted bombs and one 500lb bomb under the fuselage.

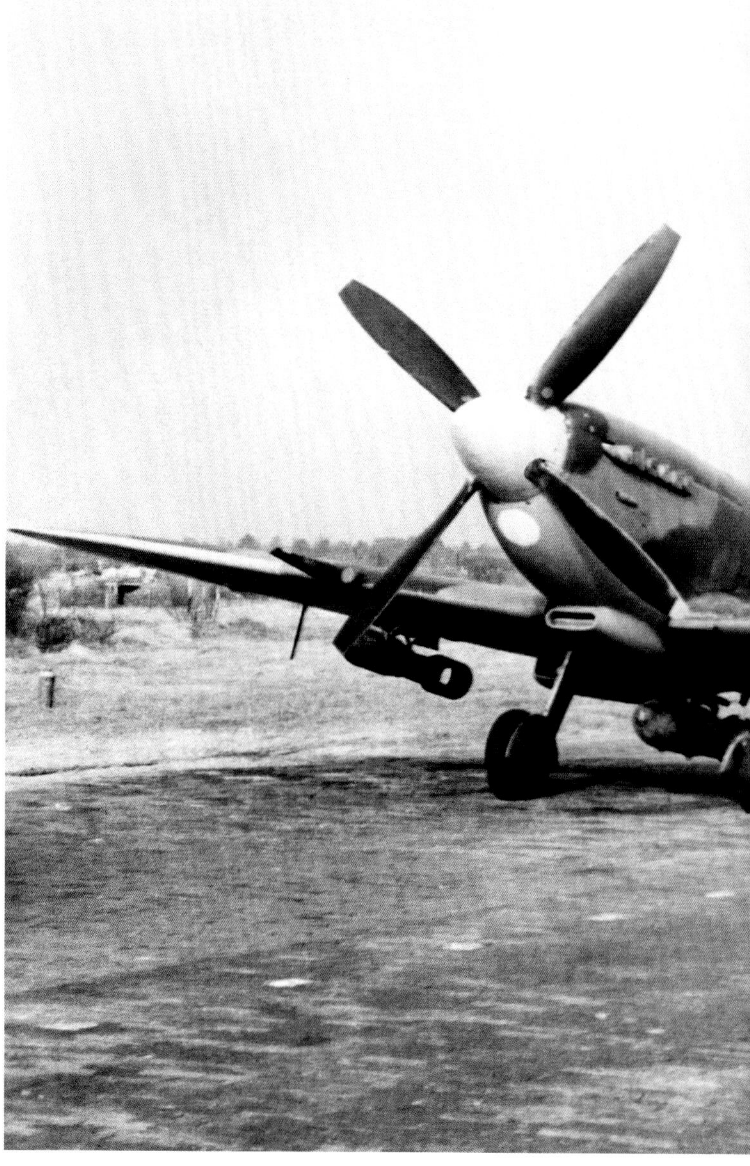

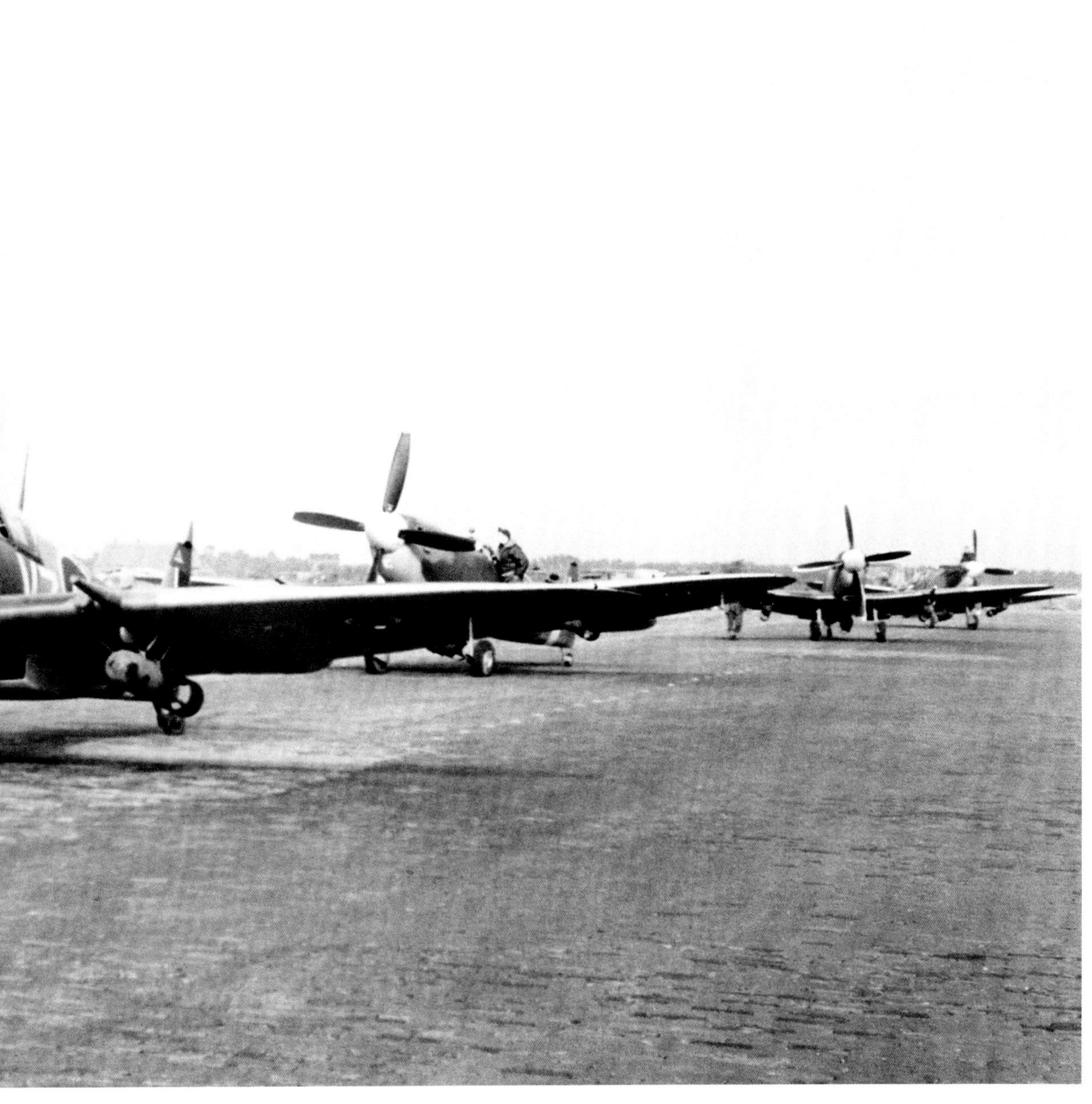

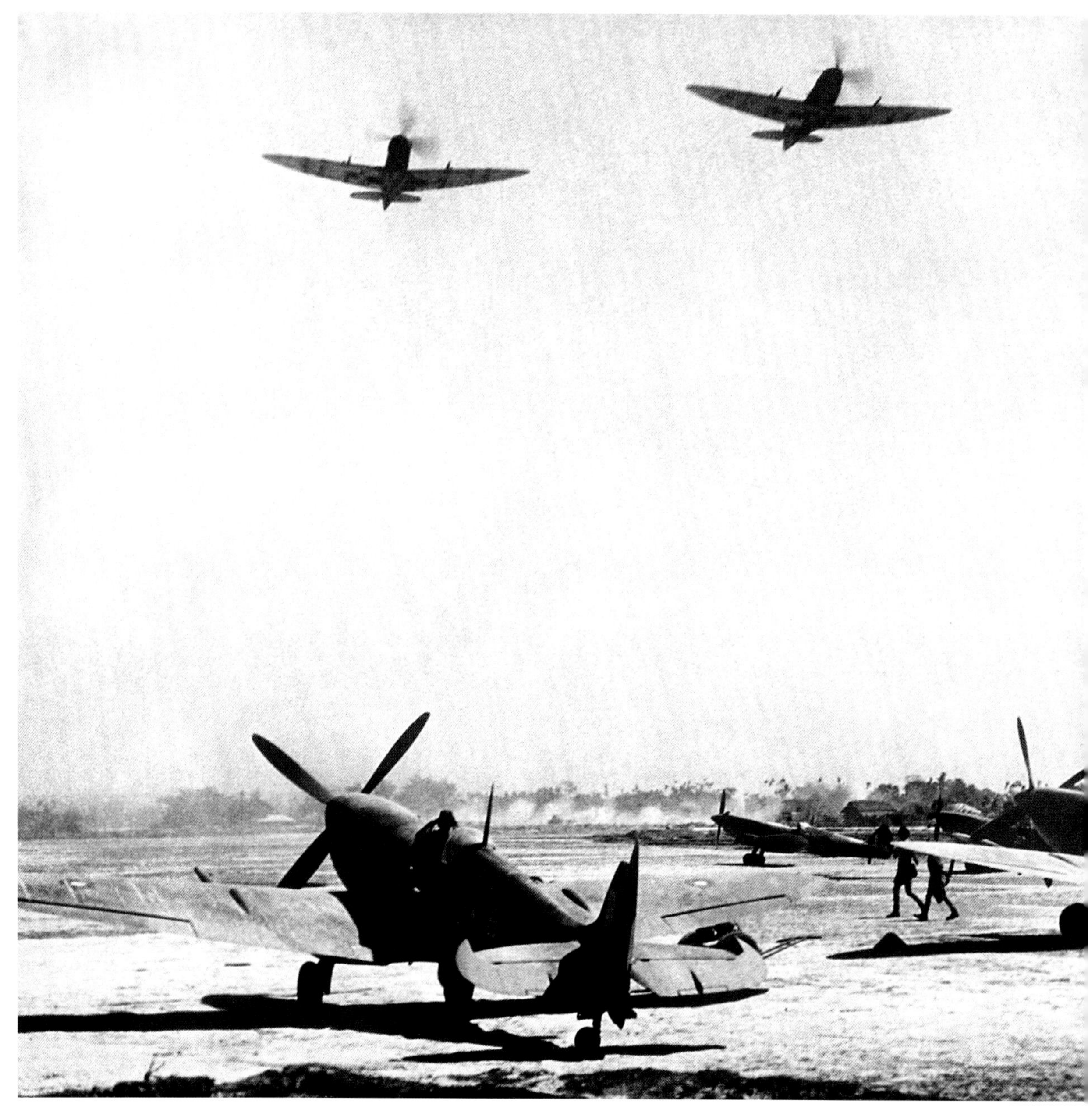

Three Spitfire Mk VIII's of 136 Squadron flying over other Mk VIII's on an airfield in northern Burma, early 1944. Originally intended as the RAF's answer to the Focke-Wulf Fw 190, the Mk VIII featured a redesigned and strengthened airframe that could hold the newer two-stage supercharged Merlin engines.

A ground crewman helps a pilot of 601 Squadron into the cockpit of his Spitfire Mk VIII at Venafro, Italy, before an offensive sweep, May 1944. The Mk VIII (and VII) introduced an extended elevator and a larger, pointed rudder that helped improve control and stability.

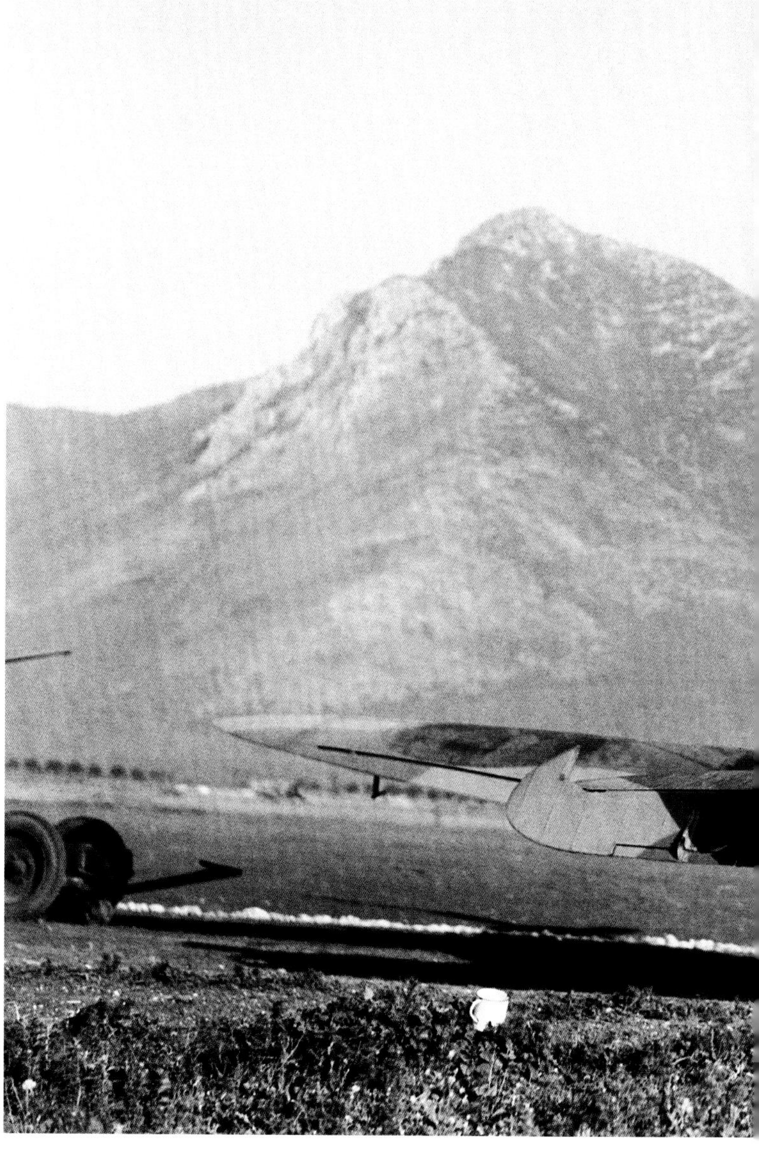

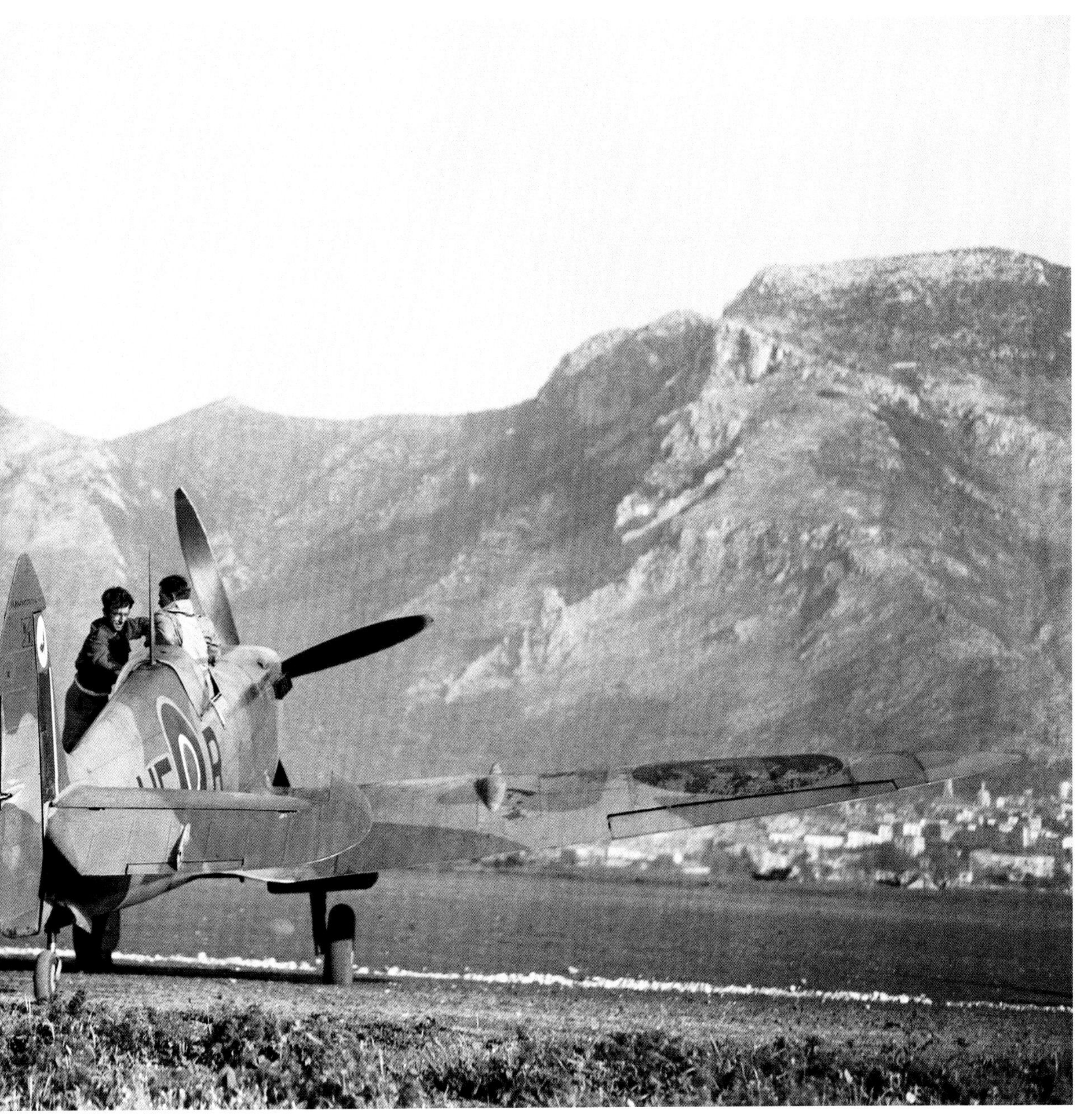

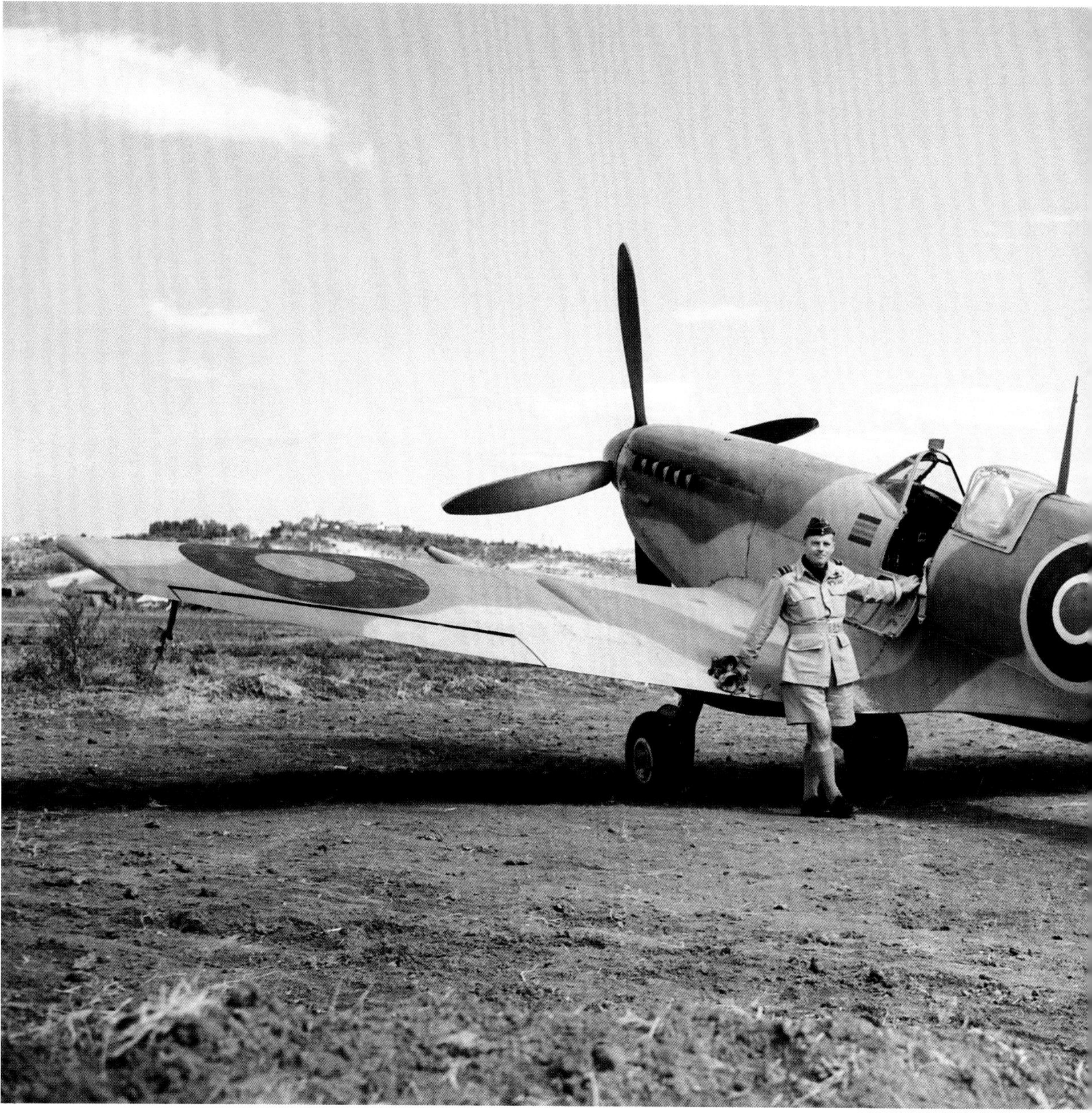

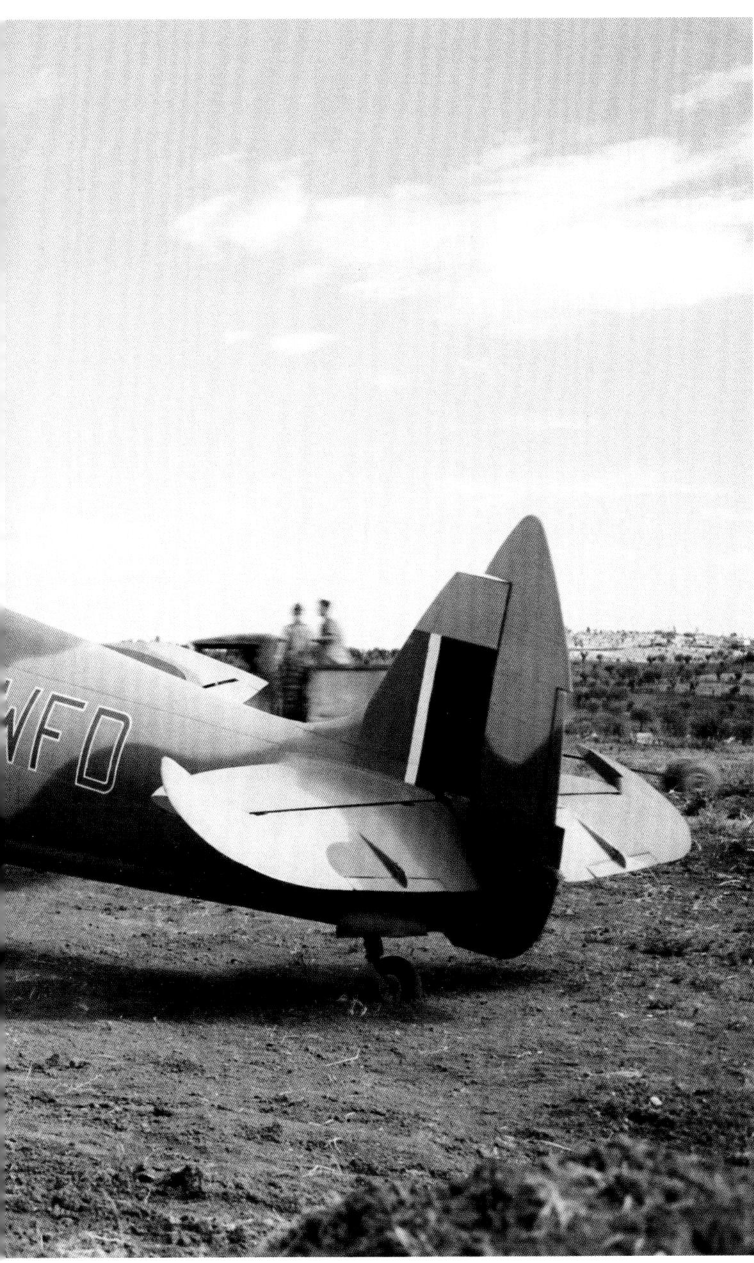

Air Vice Marshal William F Dickson with his personal Spitfire LF Mk VIII, JF814 'WFD', in northern Italy, October 1944. Powered by the Merlin 66 engine, the 'low flying' Mk VIII variant performed best at lower altitudes, with clipped wings to increase roll rate.

Spitfire Mk VIII's and personnel of 136 Squadron lined up on a perforated steel planking (PSP) airstrip on Brown's West Island, Cocos Islands, in the Indian Ocean, August 1945. Because the 'temporary' Mk IX had established itself over Britain and western Europe, most Mk VIII's were sent to the Mediterranean, India and Burma.

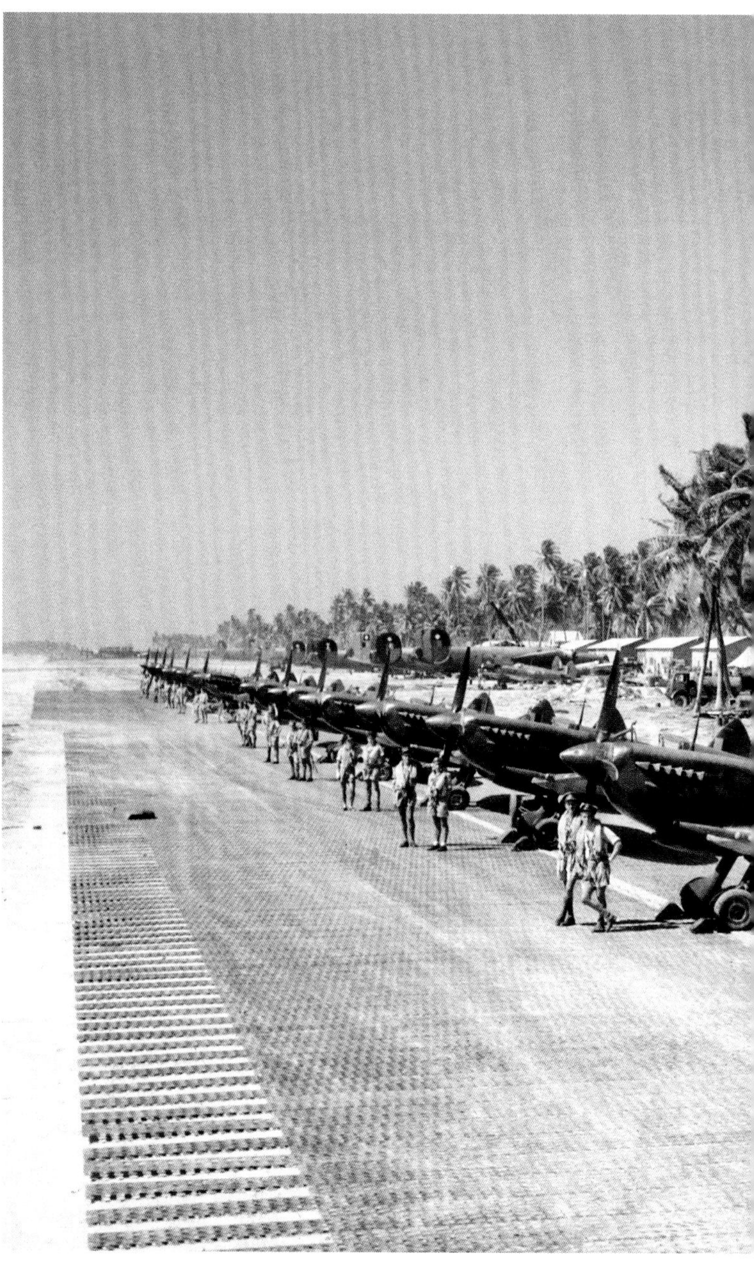

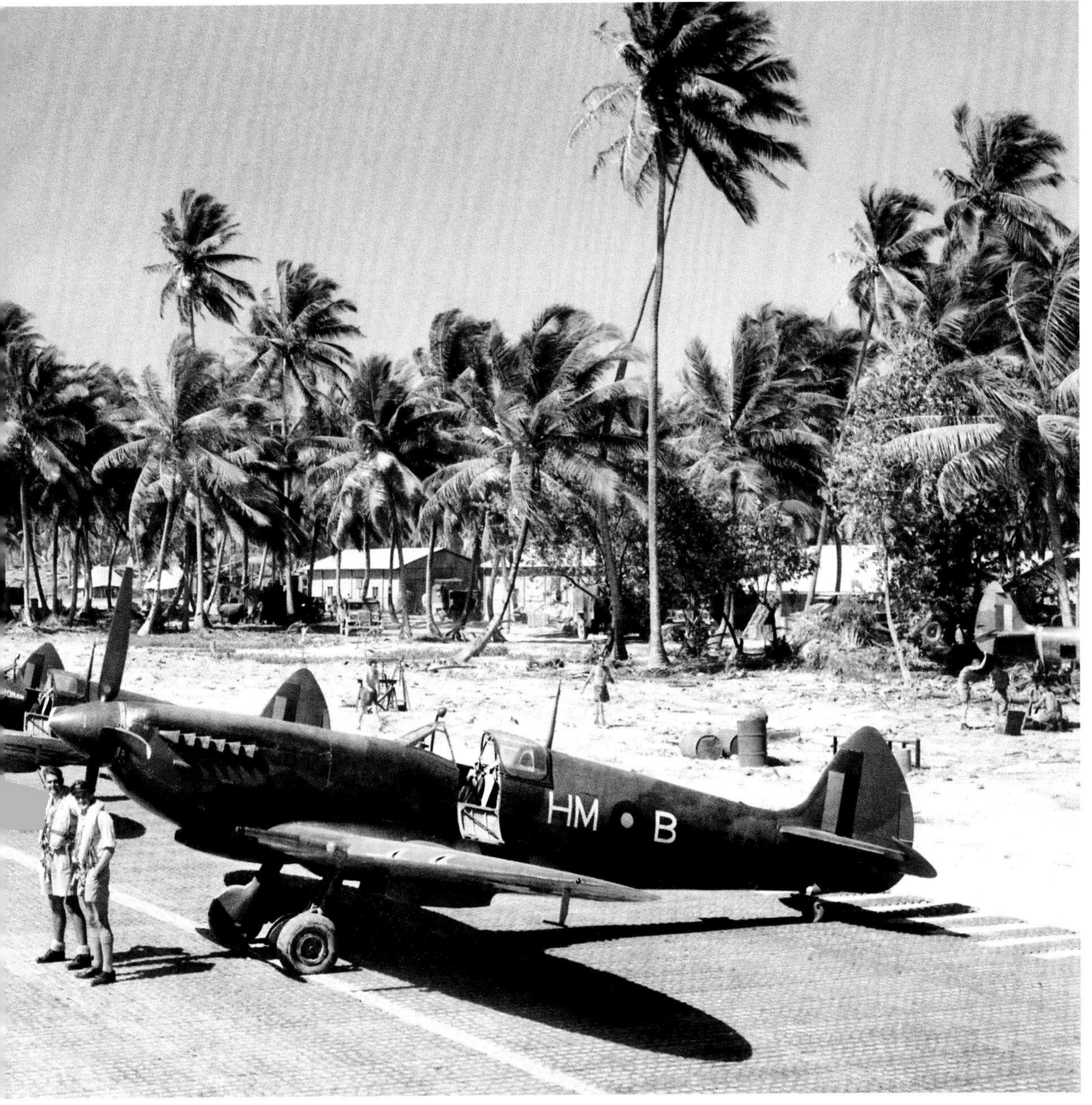
HM • B

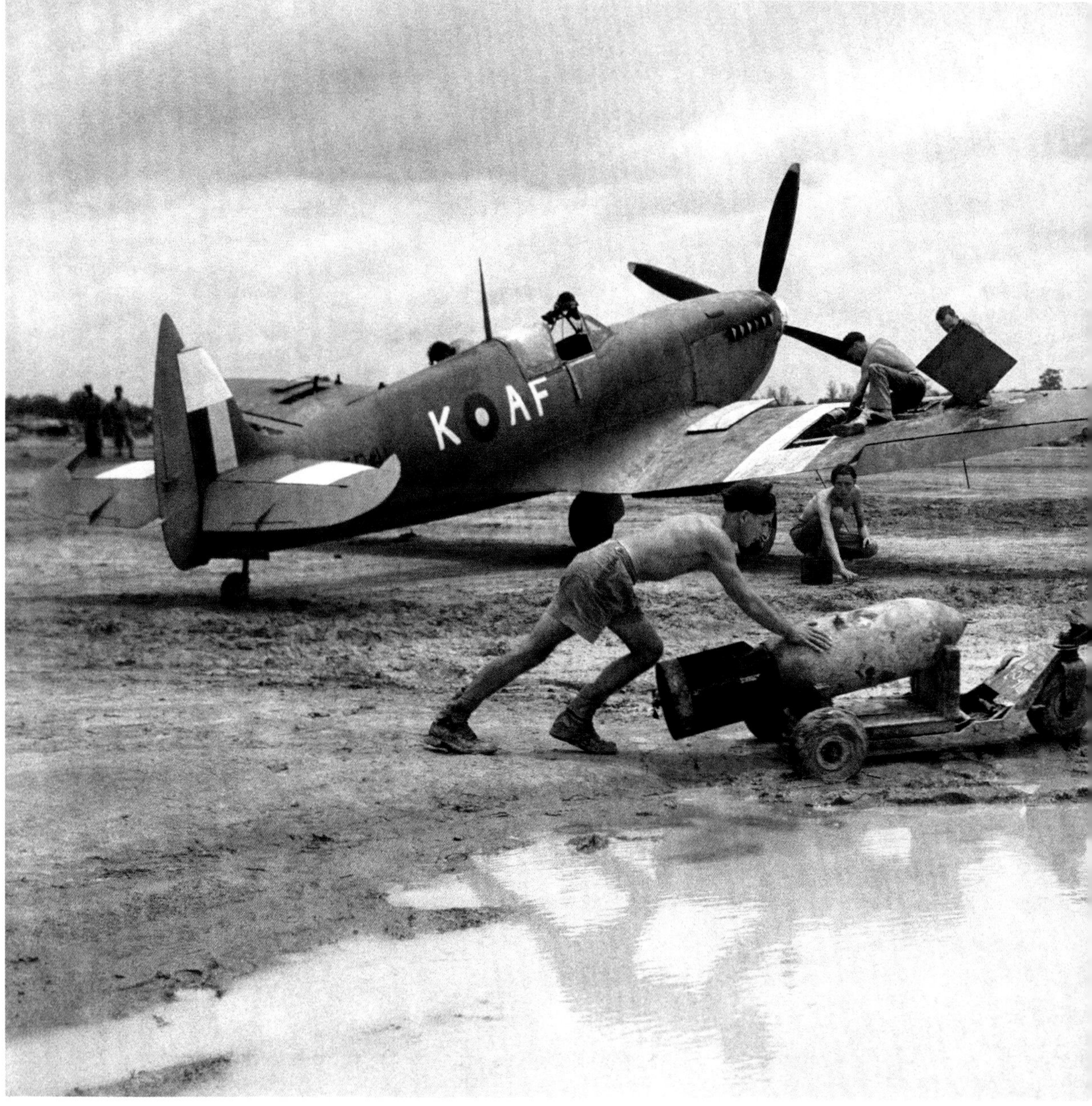
K AF

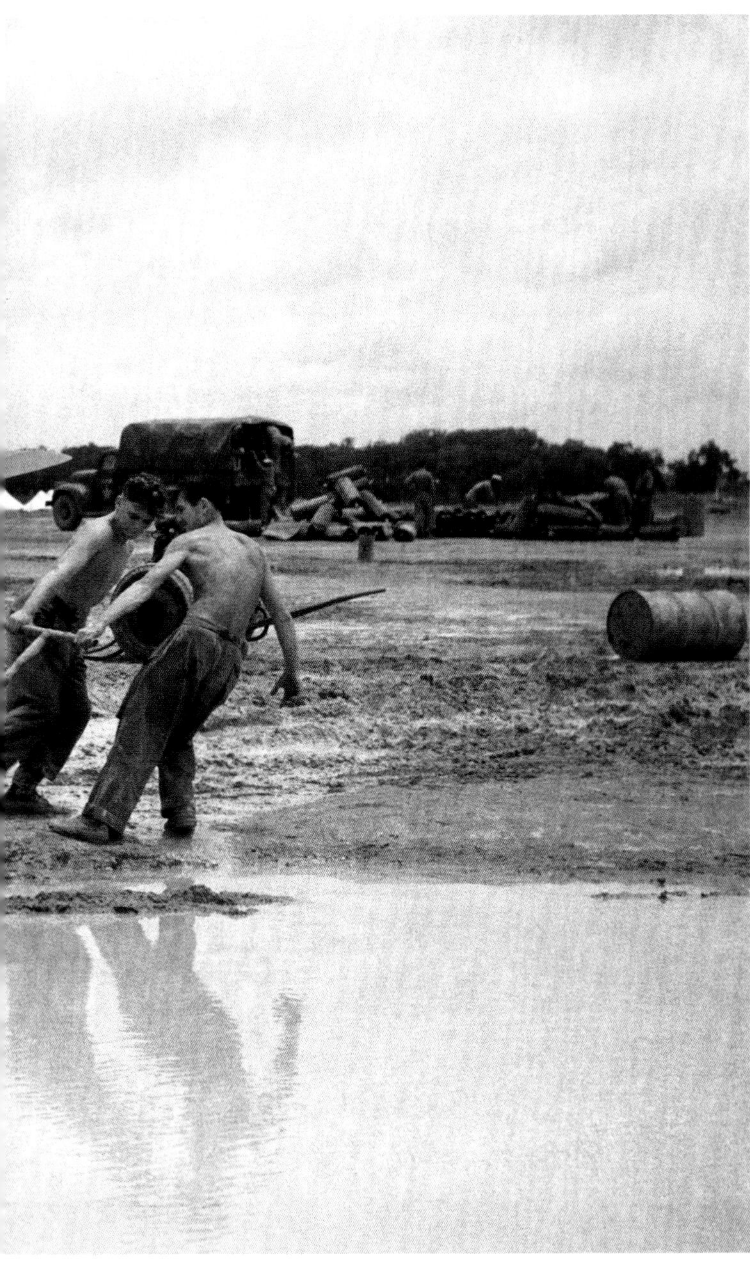

Airmen prepare a Spitfire Mk VIII of 607 Squadron for a sortie in monsoon conditions at Mingaladon, Burma, August 1945. In the India-Burma theatre, Spitfires were frequently used for ground attack operations against Japanese targets.

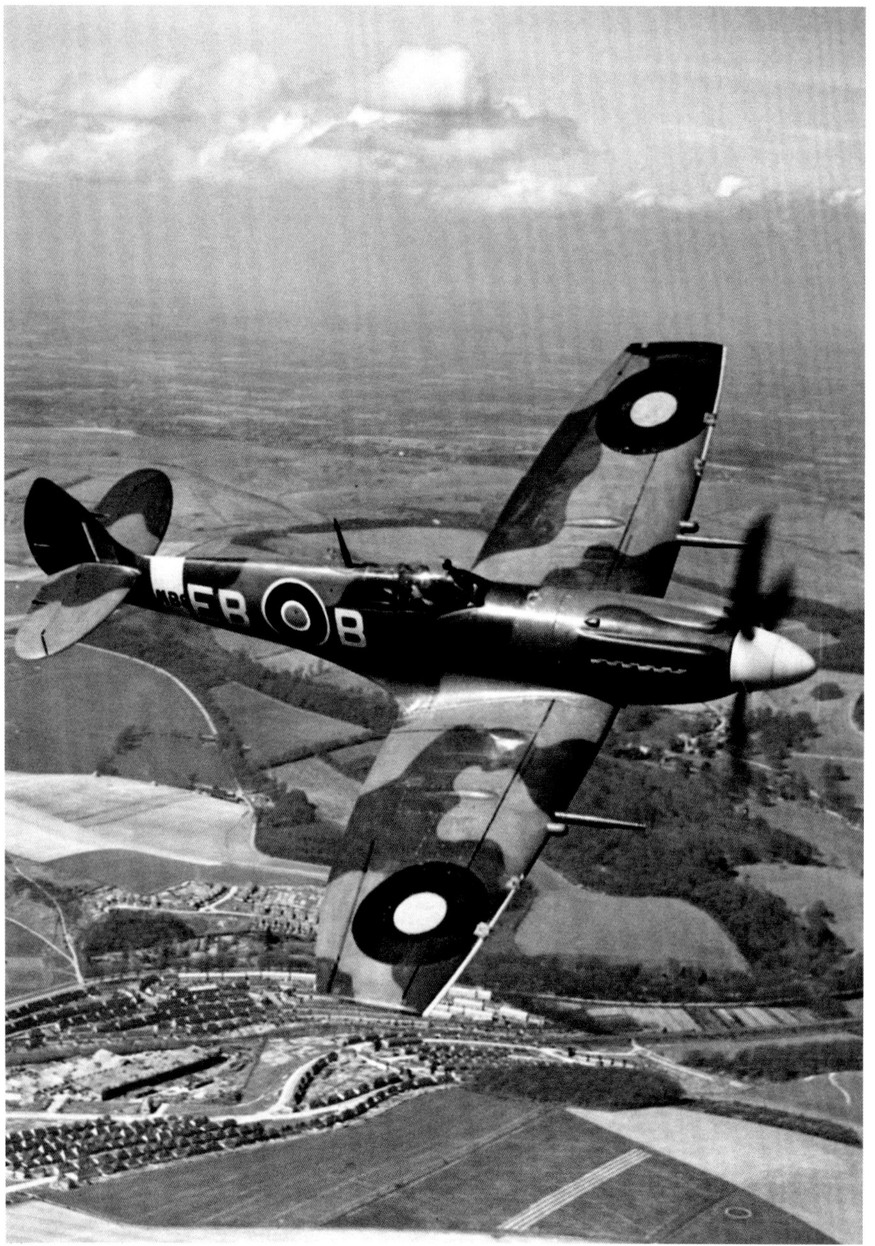

Spitfire Mk XII, MB882 'EB-B', of 41 Squadron banking to starboard, April 1944. The Mk XII was the first production Spitfire to be powered by the Rolls Royce Griffon series of engines, which dramatically increased its power.

The underside of Spitfire Mk XII MB882, showing the retracted wheels, April 1944. Because the single-stage supercharged Griffon engines gave their best performance at lower altitudes, all Mk XII Spitfires featured clipped wingtips to increase roll rate.

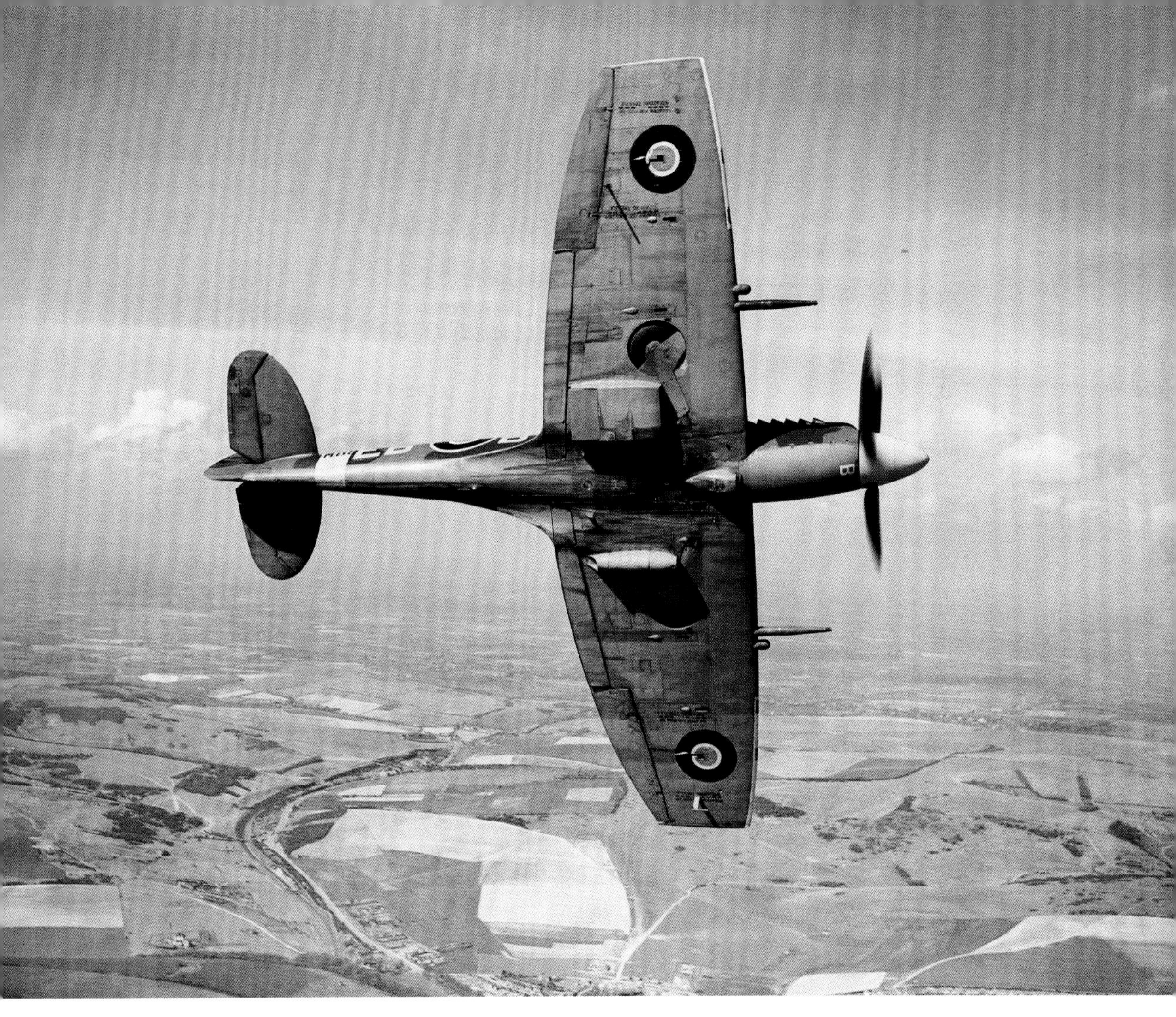

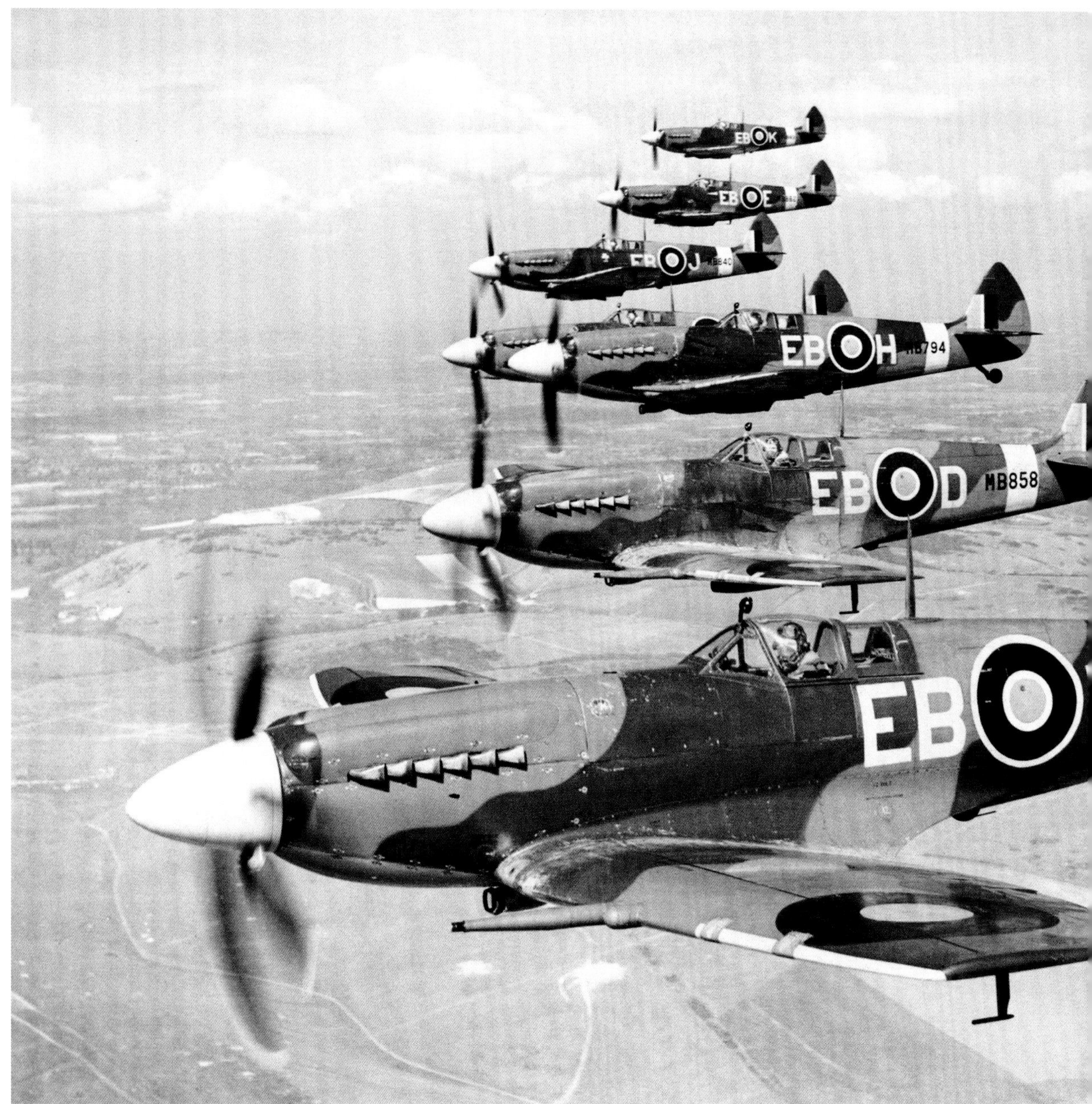

EB K
EB E
EB J
EB H MB794
EB D MB858
EB

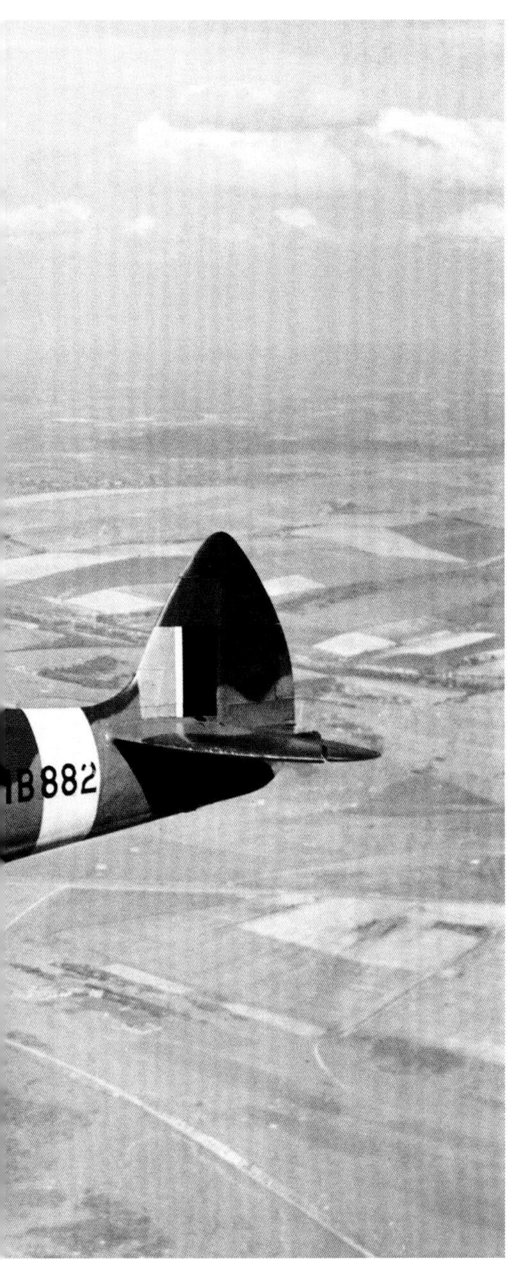

Seven Spitfire Mk XII's (MB882 'EB-B', nearest) of 41 Squadron based at Friston, Sussex, in flight over the South Downs, April 1944. Although excellent at lower altitudes, the Mk XII's performance dropped off at higher altitudes due to its single-stage supercharged engine.

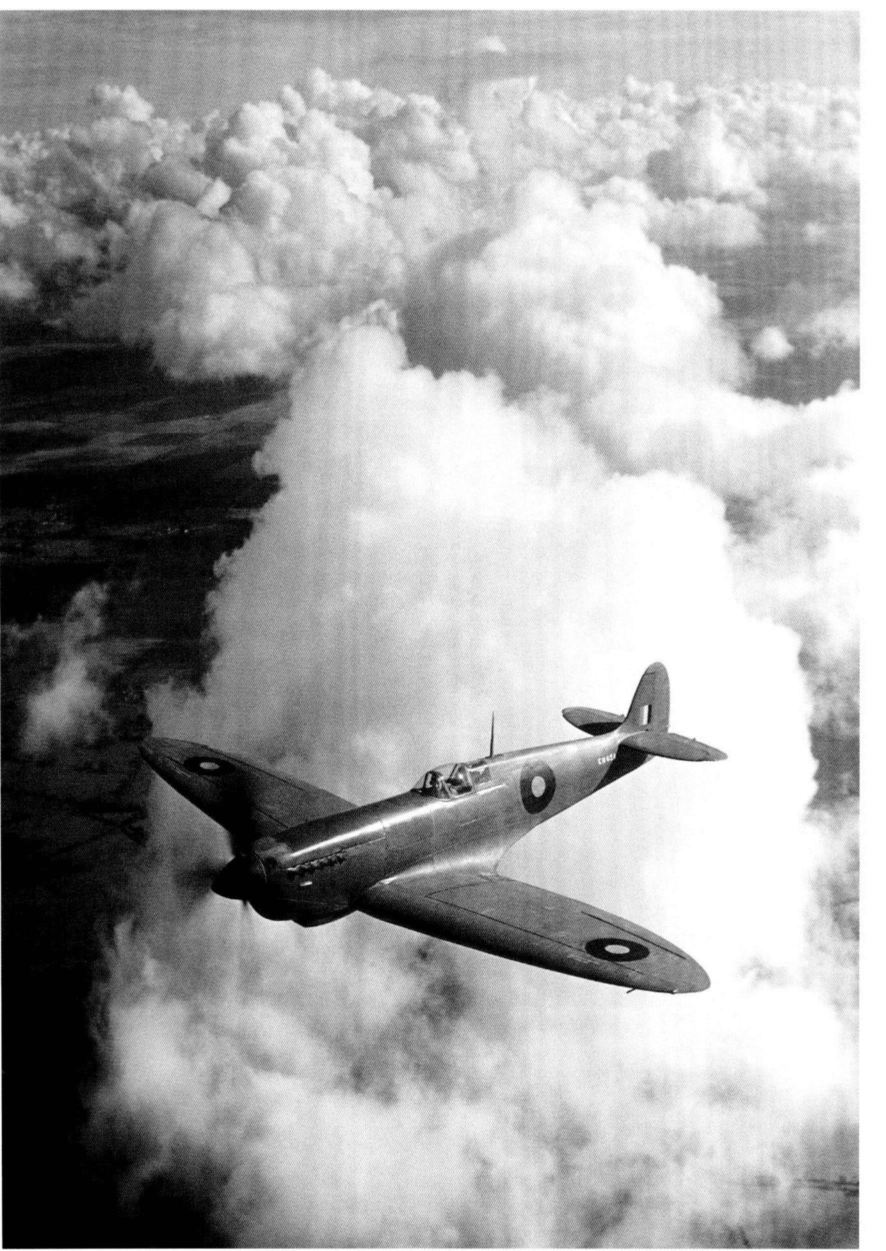

Spitfire PR Mk XI, EN654, on a test flight, 1943. The Mk XI was the most produced of the numerous photo reconaissance (PR) variants. Armed with cameras instead of guns, PR Spitfires were designed to fly far enough to reach enemy territory and fast enough to evade enemy defences.

Spitfire Mk XIVC of 610 Squadron in flight, July 1944. The Mk XIV introduced the two-stage supercharged Griffon 65 engine, which resulted in a vast improvement in performance over both the Mk IX and the Mk XII at all altitudes.

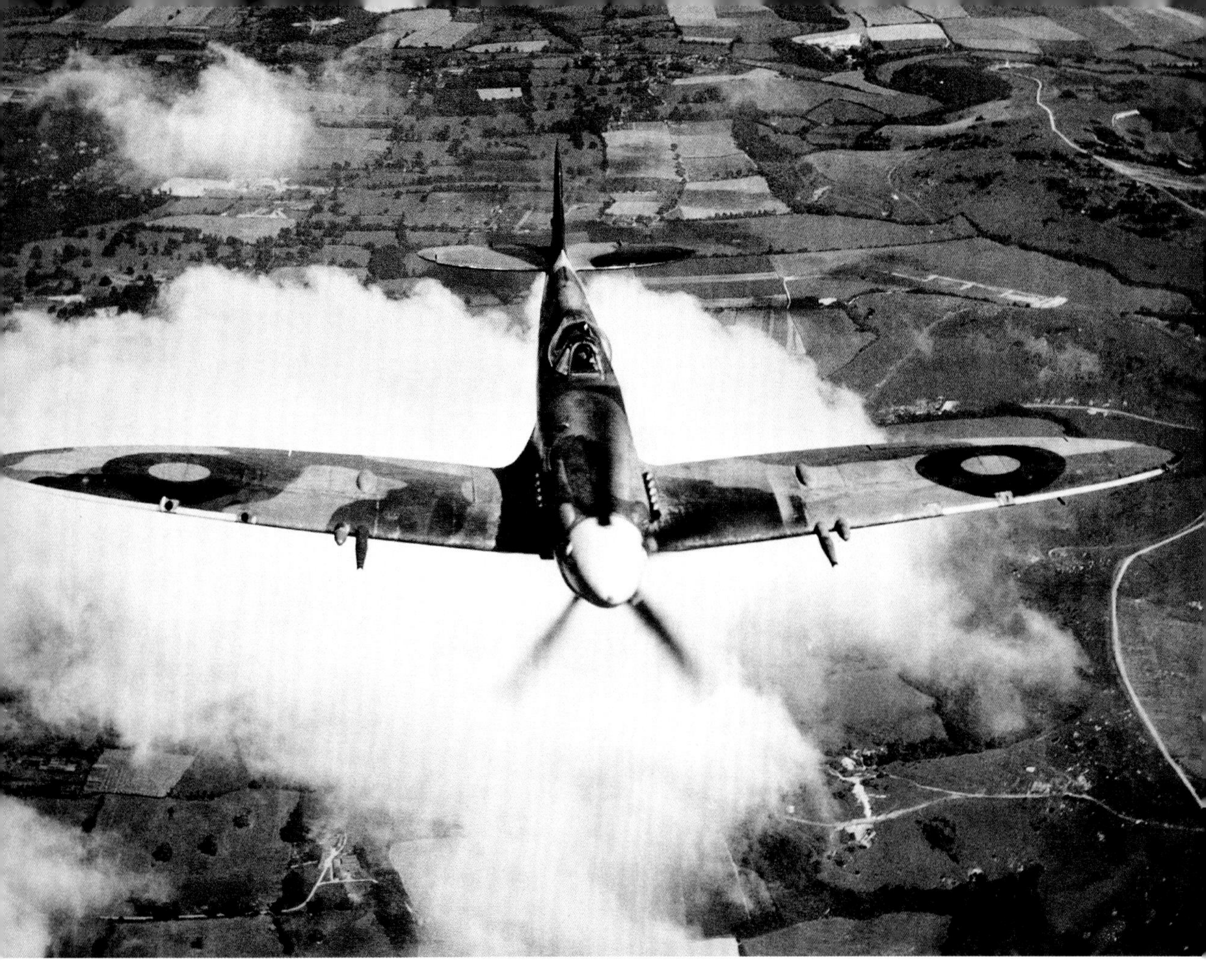

Four Spitfire XIVC's of 610 Squadron, based at Friston, Sussex, flying in formation over south-east England, July 1944. Capable of speeds up to 446mph, the Mk XIV was fast enough to catch V1 flying bombs headed for England and was the most successful Spitfire at destroying them.

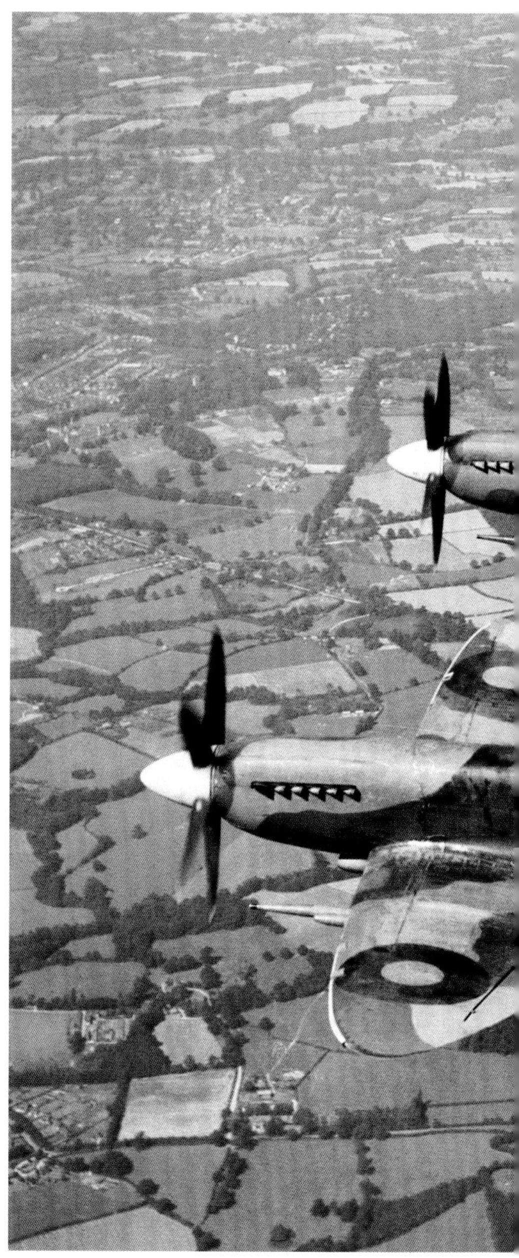

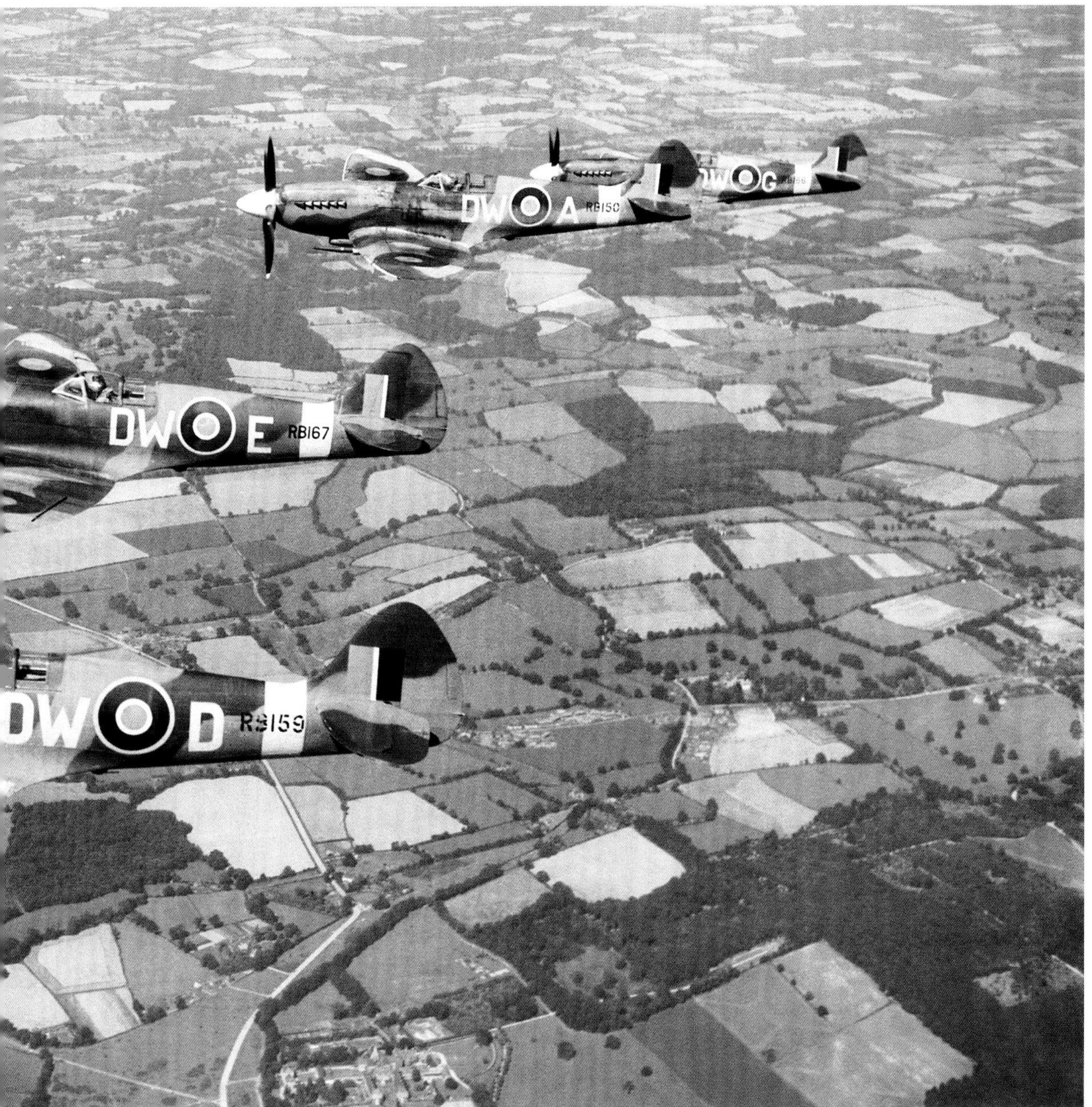
DW A
RB150
DW G
DW E
RB167
DW D
RB159

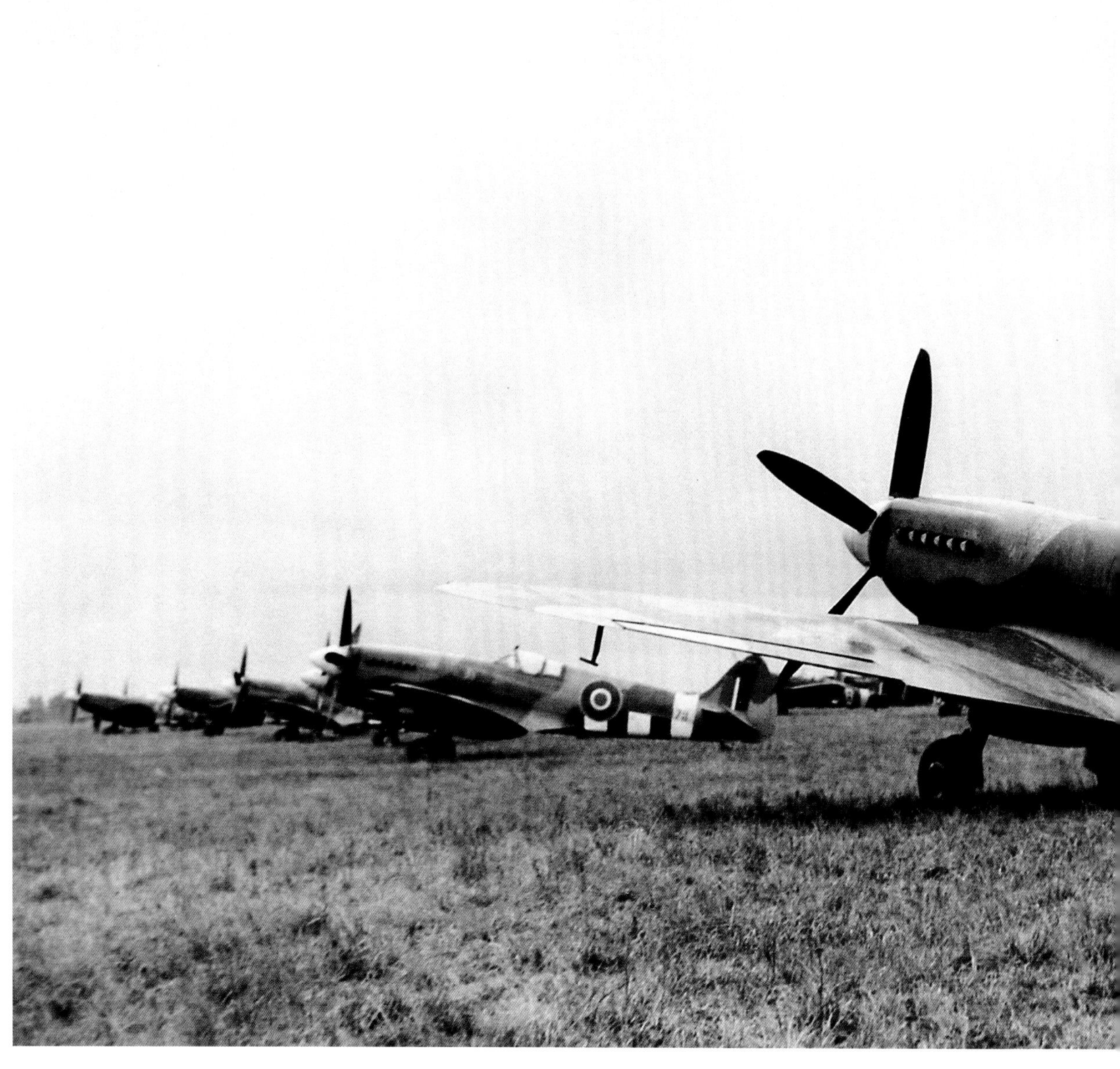

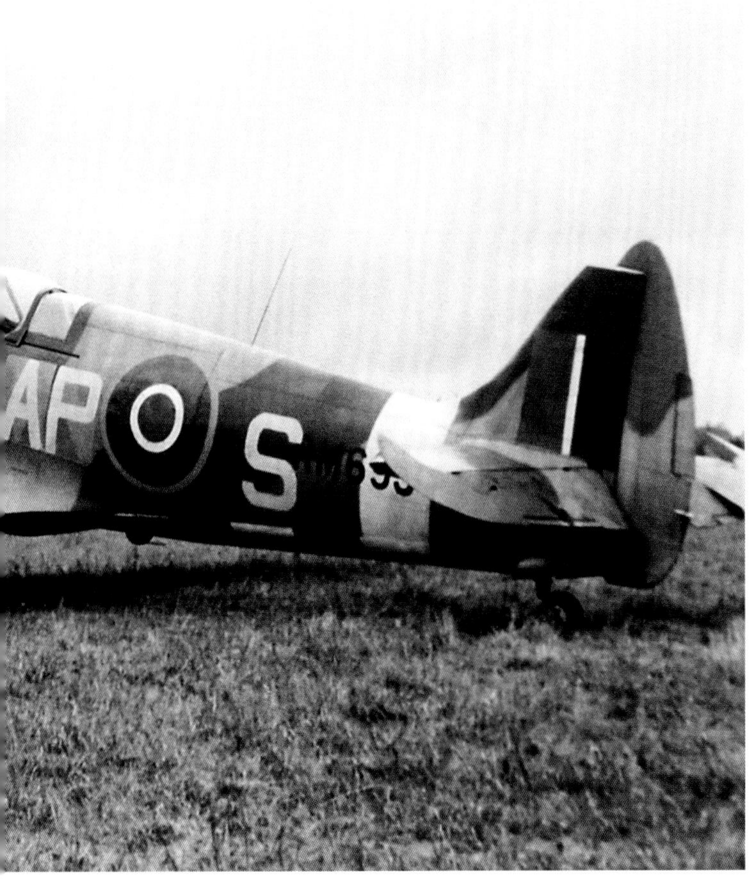

Spitfire Mk XIV's (RM693 'AP-S', nearest) of 130 Squadron, on the ground at Grave, Holland, October 1944. With a longer nose to accommodate the larger Griffon engine, the Mk XIV also had a five-bladed propeller and a larger fin and rudder to counter the increased torque.

Ground staff prepare Spitfire XIVE, RN187 'FF-U', of 132 Squadron, newly off-loaded from the carrier HMS *Vindex* at Iwakuni, Japan, September 1946. The Mk XIV ended the Second World War as arguably the best Spitfire mark to see extensive service.

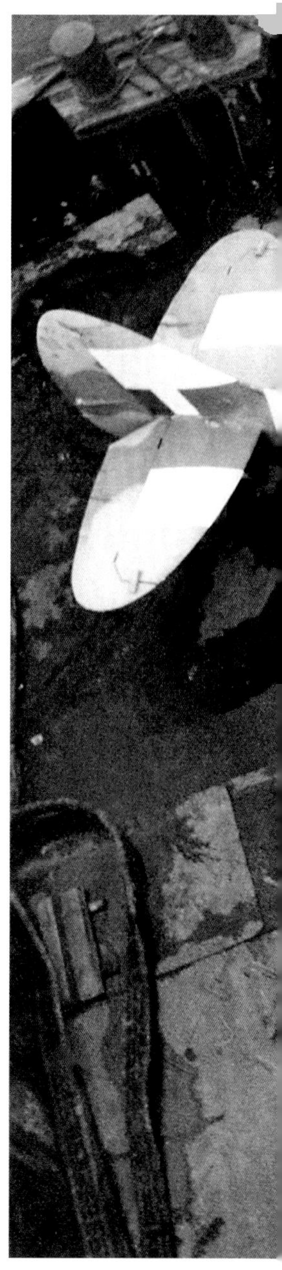

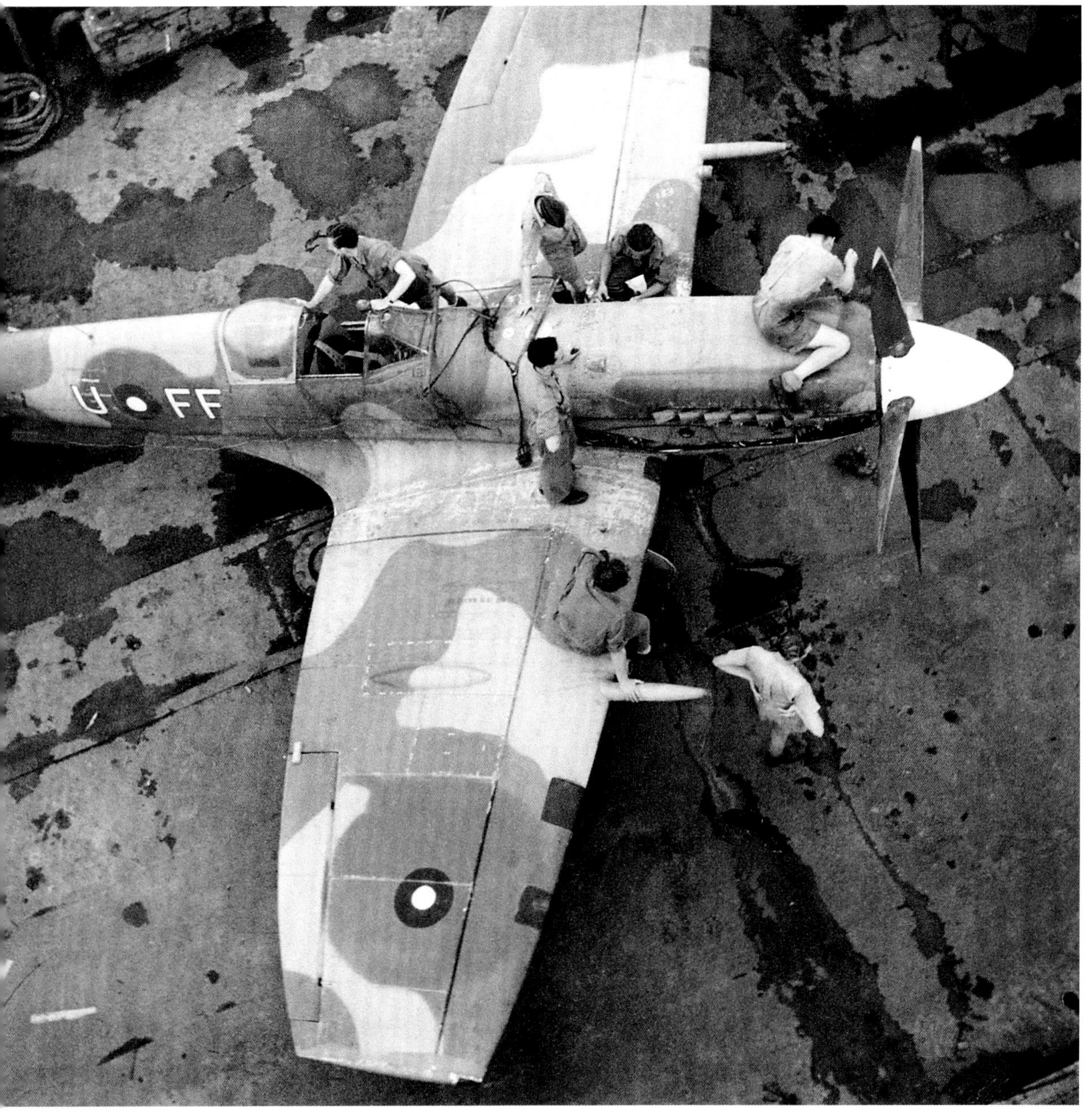
U FF

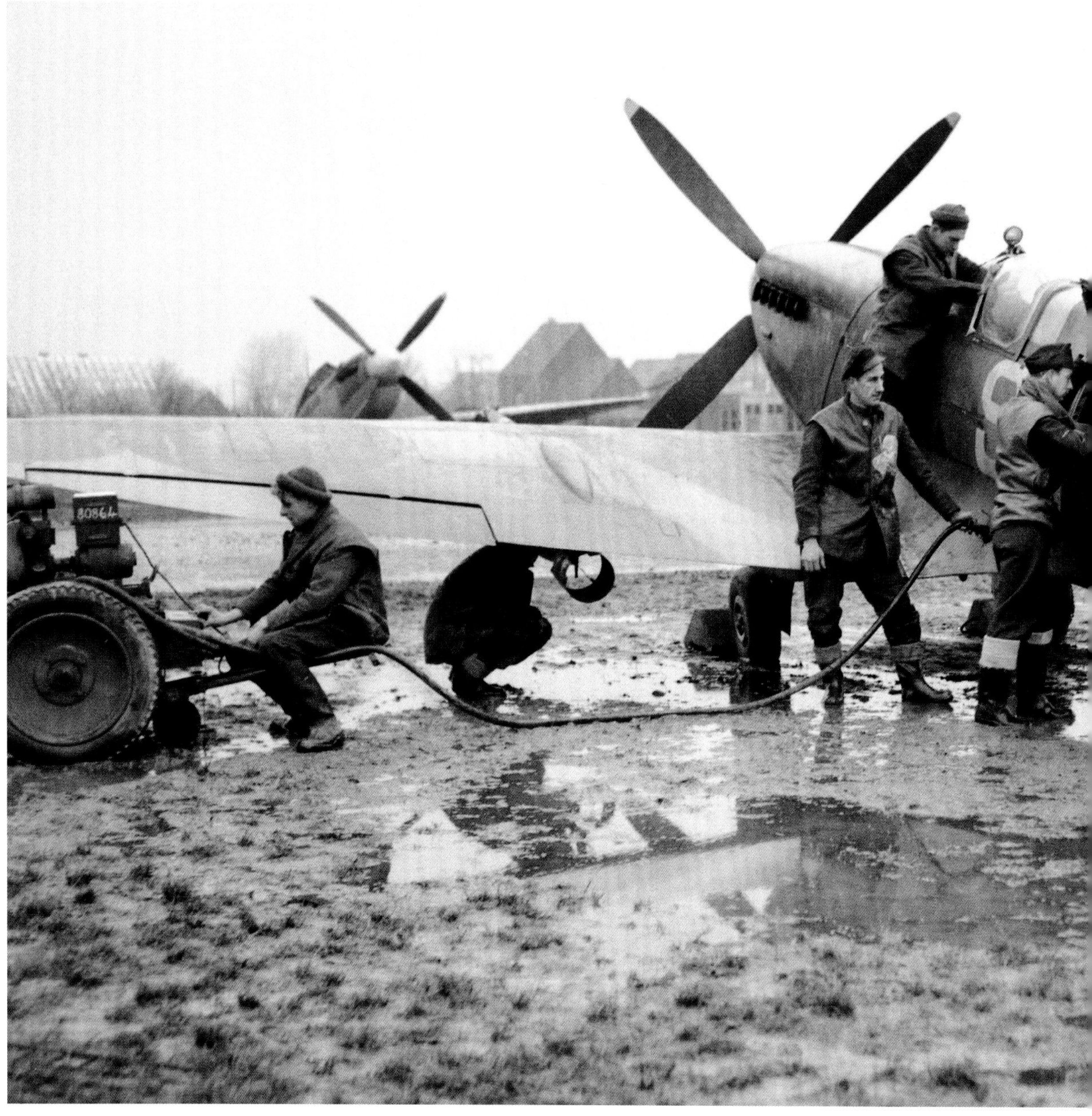
80864

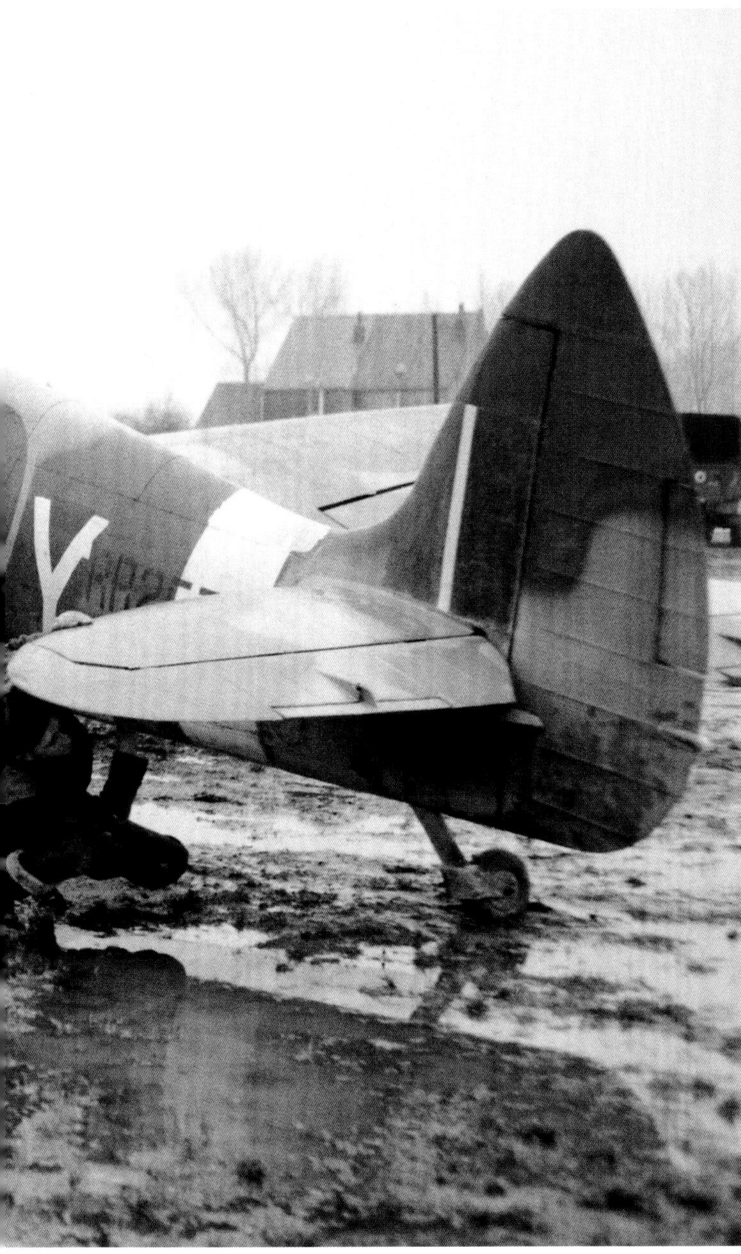

Ground crew carry out an inspection of Spitfire Mk XVI, RR257 '9N-Y', of 127 Squadron in muddy conditions at Grimbergen, Belgium, December 1944. The XVI was very similar to the IX, but was powered by the American-built Packard Merlin 266 engine.

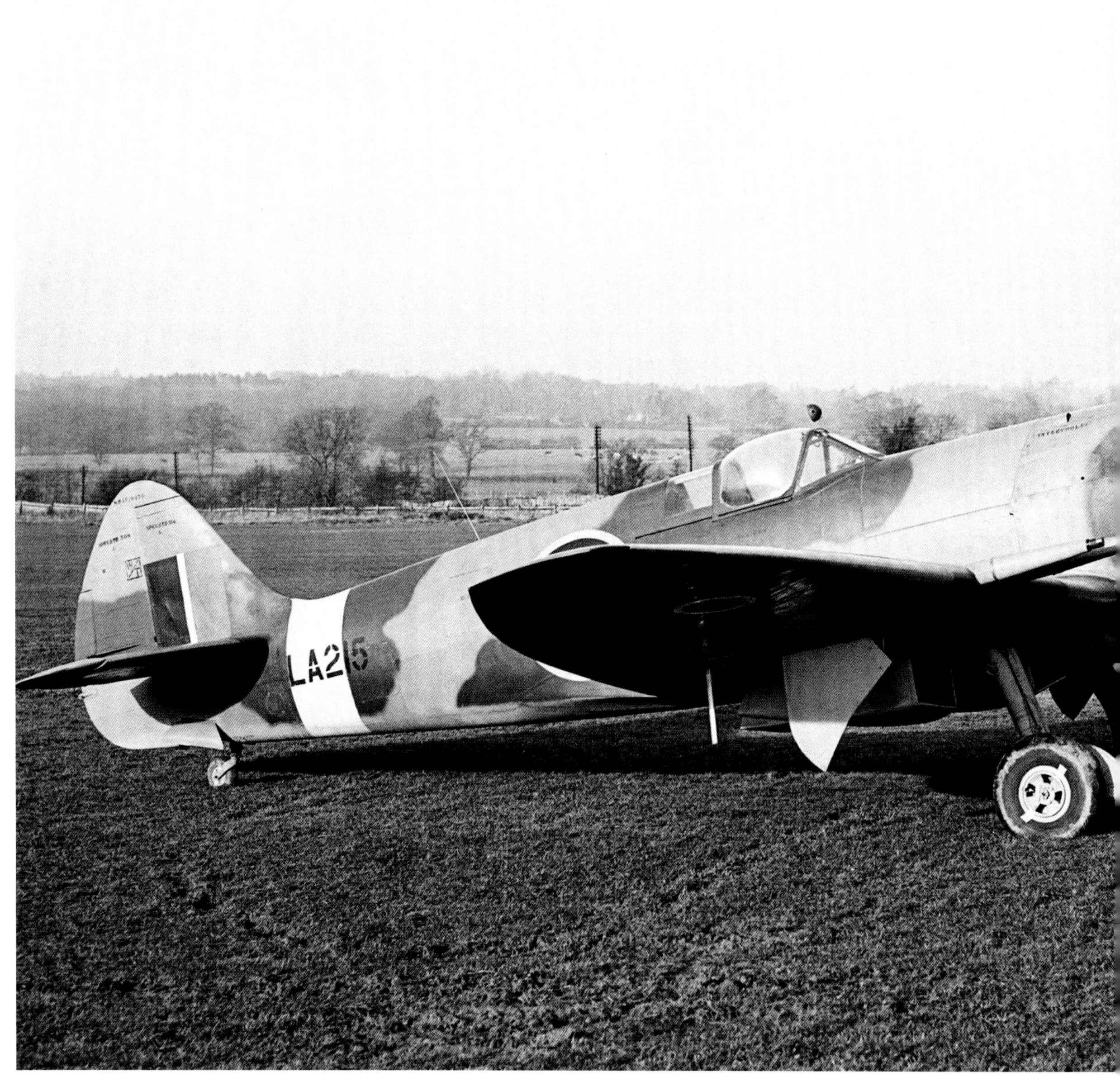
LA215

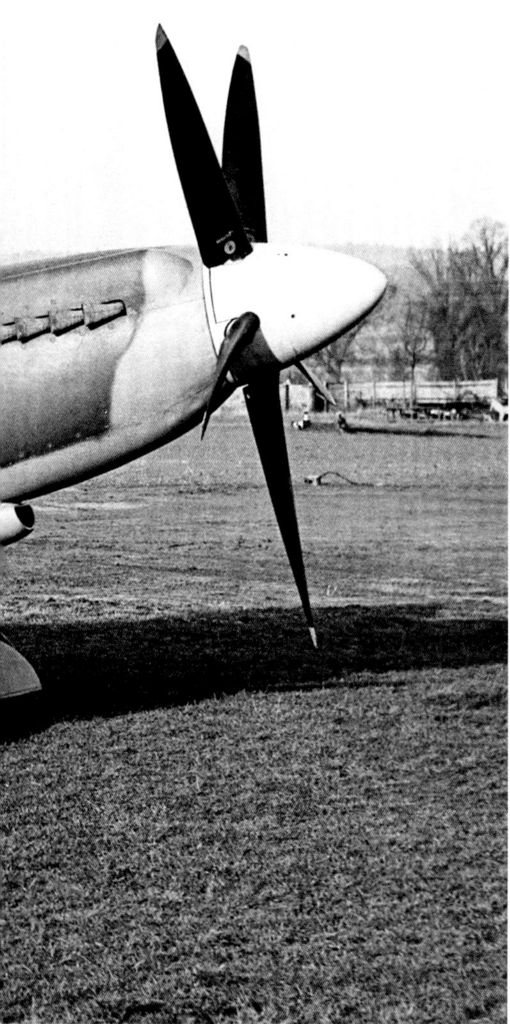

Spitfire Mk 21, LA215, ground view. Entering service towards the end of the Second World War, the Mk 21 introduced a completely redesigned and strengthened wing that could cope better with the speeds produced by the Griffon engines, as well as a larger five-bladed propeller.

Spitfire Mk 22 prototype, PK312, in flight. The Mk 22 was almost identical to the Mk 21, but featured an enlarged tail unit, cut-down rear fuselage and a 'teardrop' canopy that gave the pilot a better all-around view.

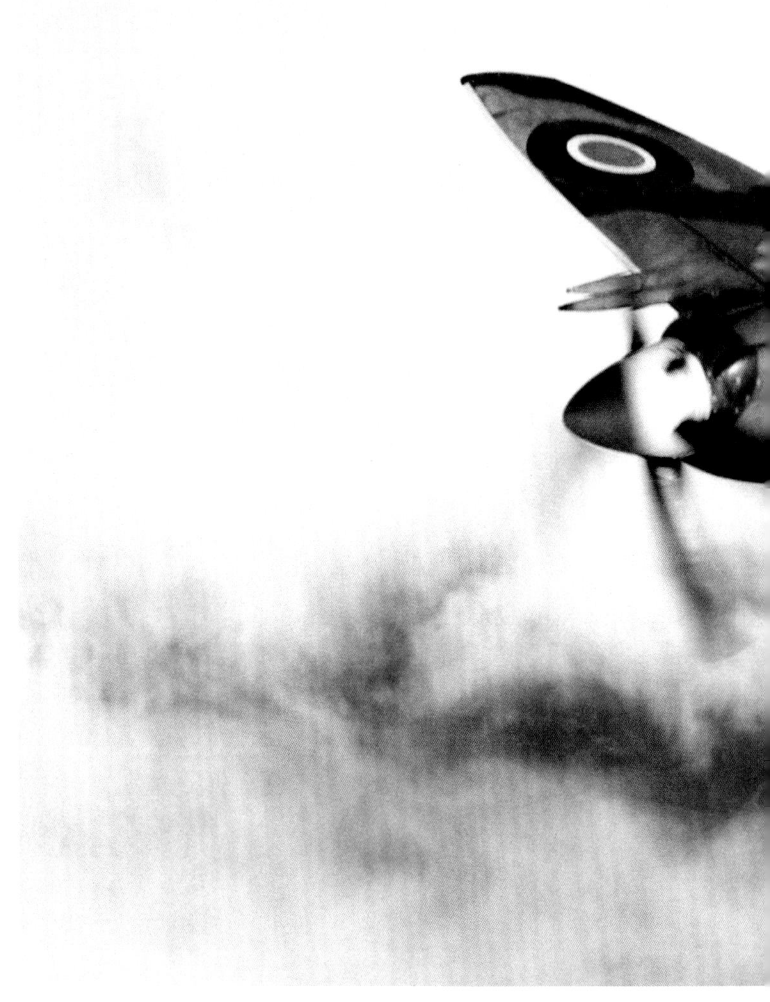

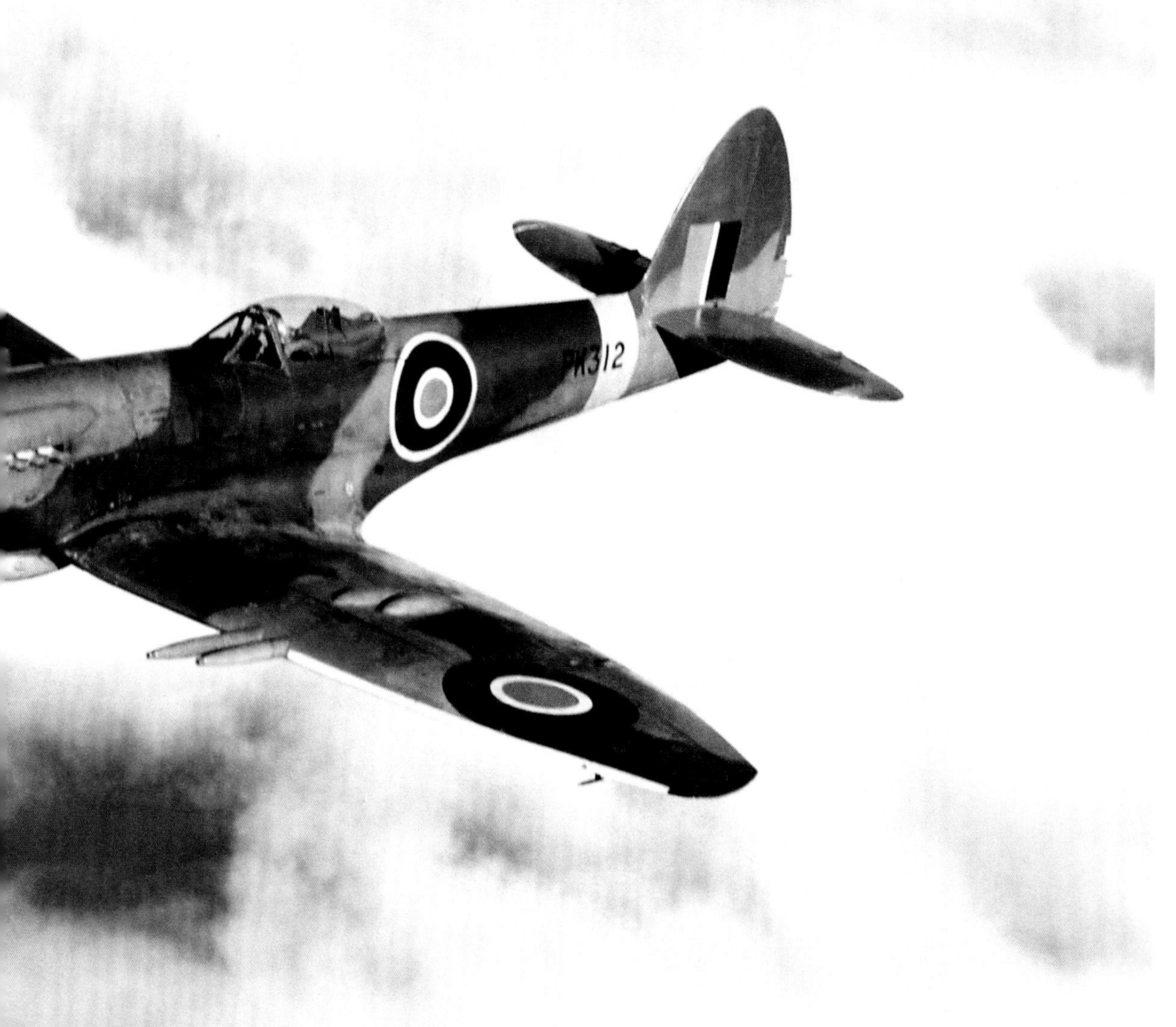
PK312

Five Spitfire Mk 24's of 80 Squadron lined up with their respective crews at RAF Guetersloh, Germany, 1948/1949. The final Spitfire mark was an improved version of the Mk 22, with increased fuel capacity. Like the Mk 21 and 22, it was armed with four 20mm cannon.

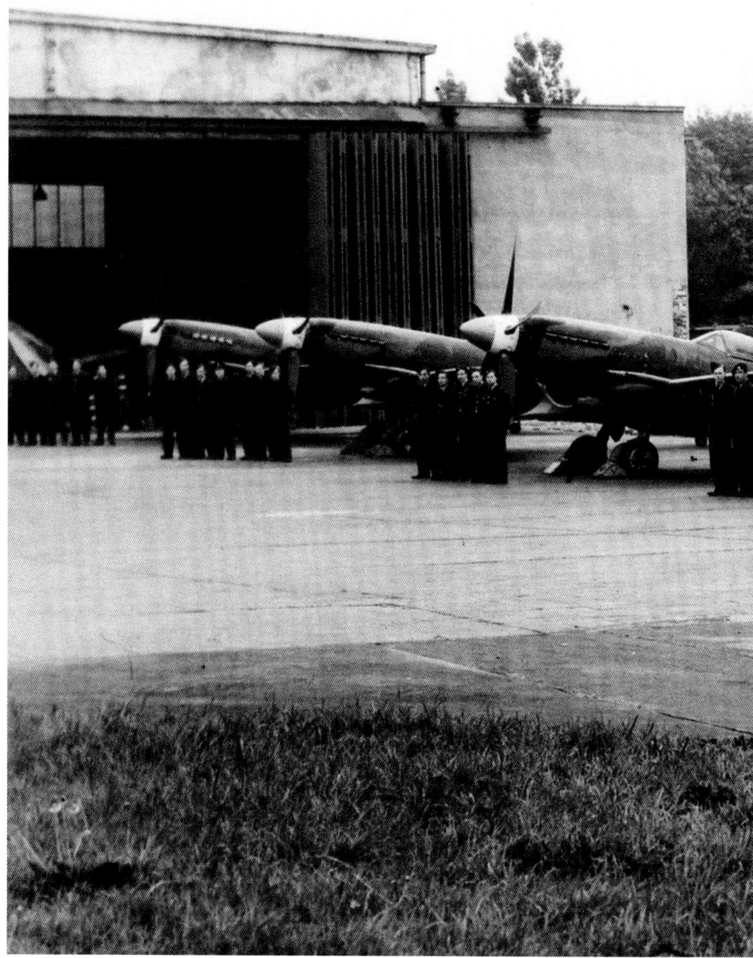

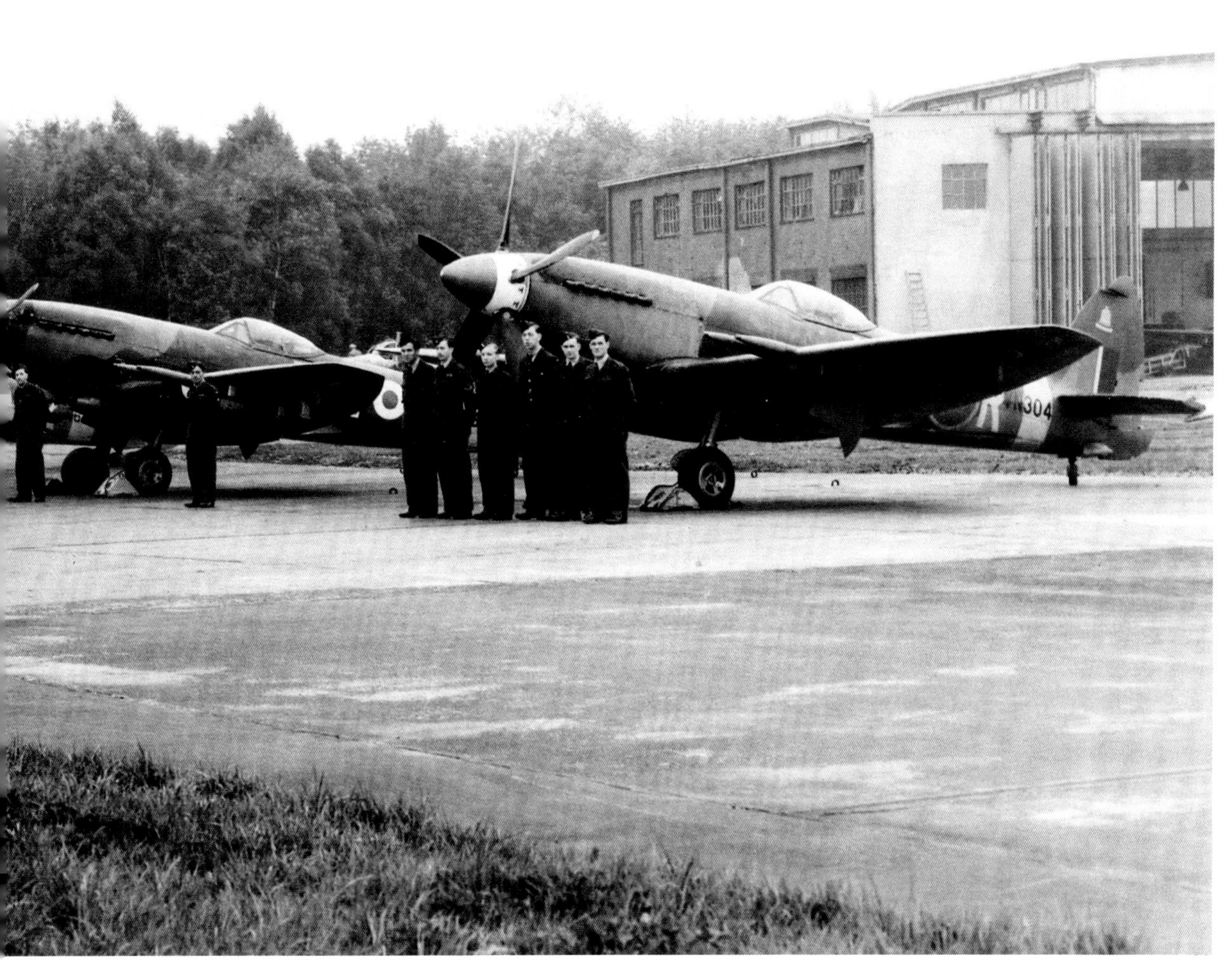

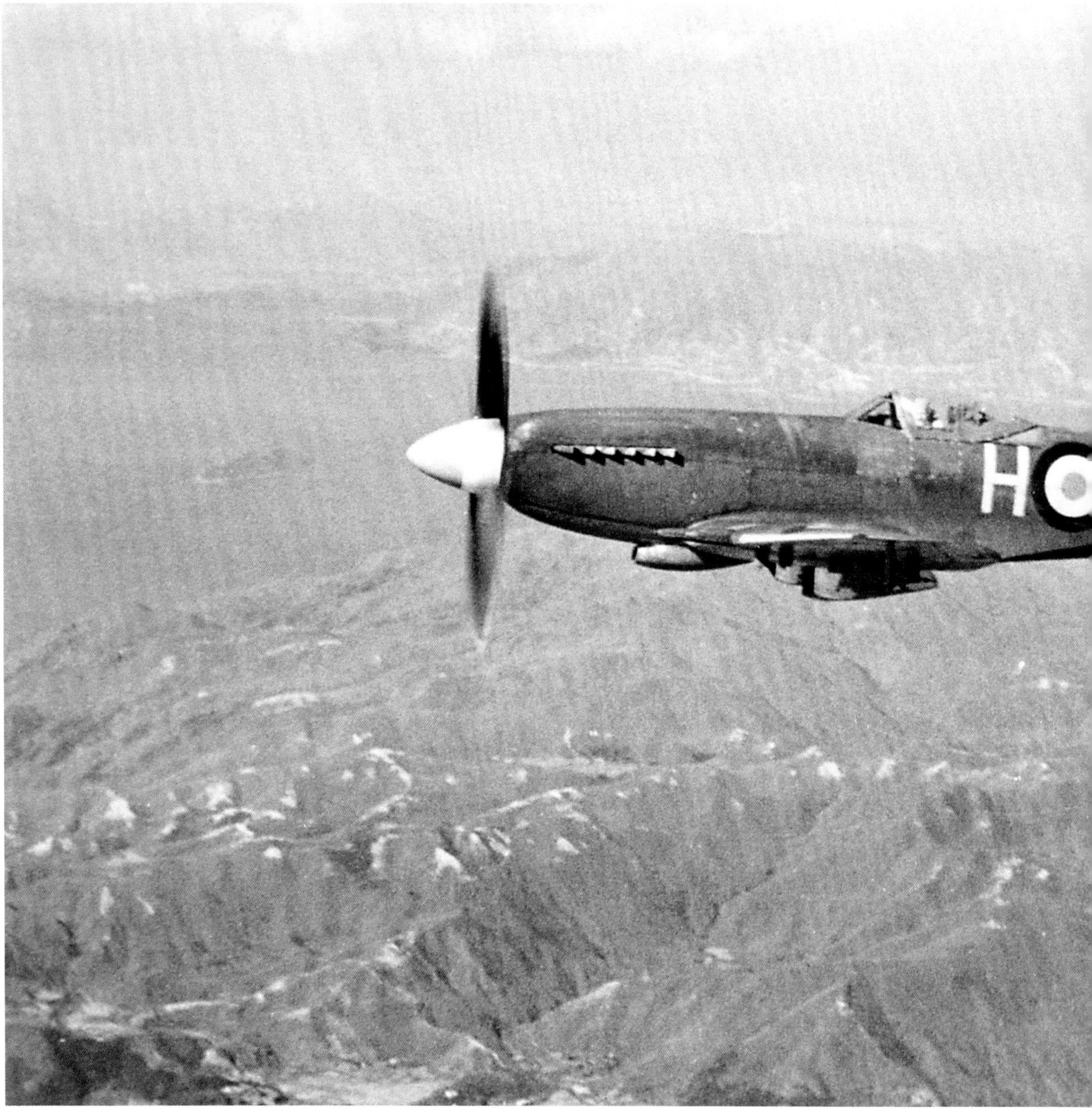

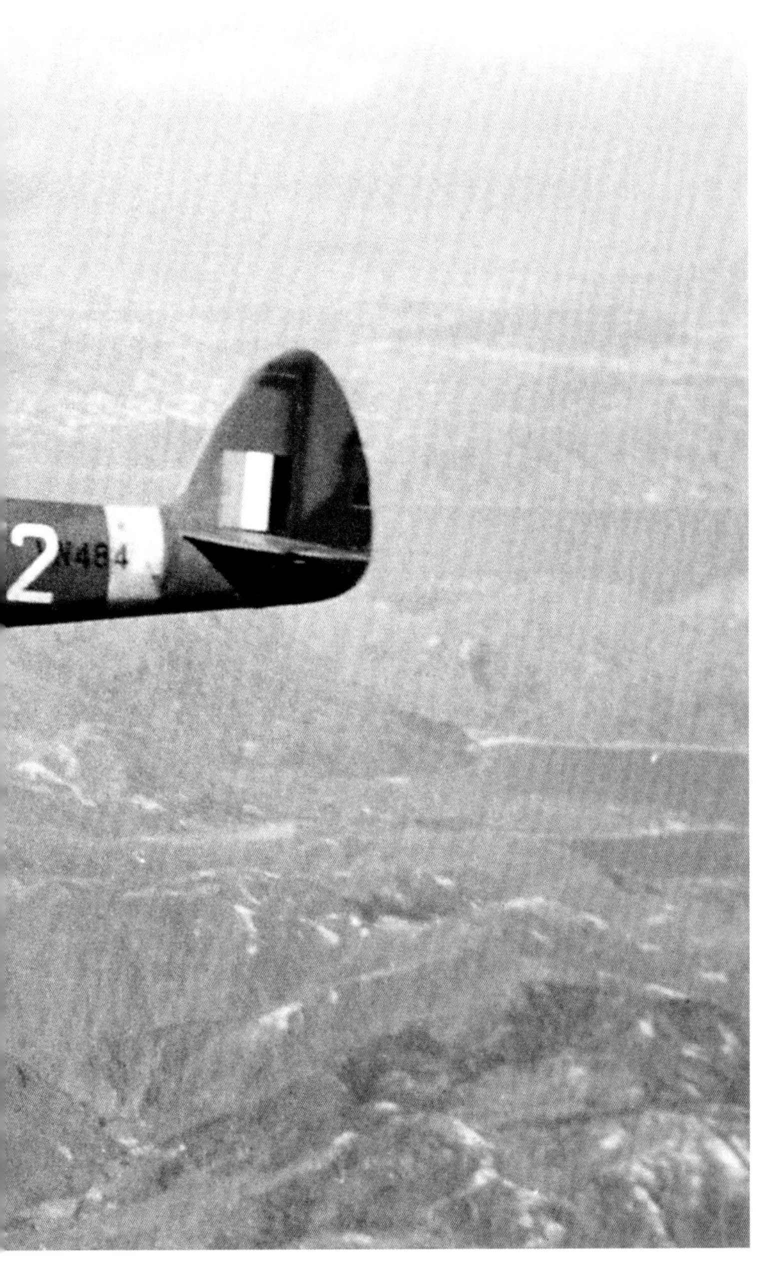

Spitfire Mk 24, VN484 'W2-H', of 80 Squadron in flight over the New Territories, Hong Kong, 1950/1951. Although the Mk 24 represented a quantum leap over the first Spitfire mark in terms of performance, only 81 were produced, with Spitfire production ending in February 1948.

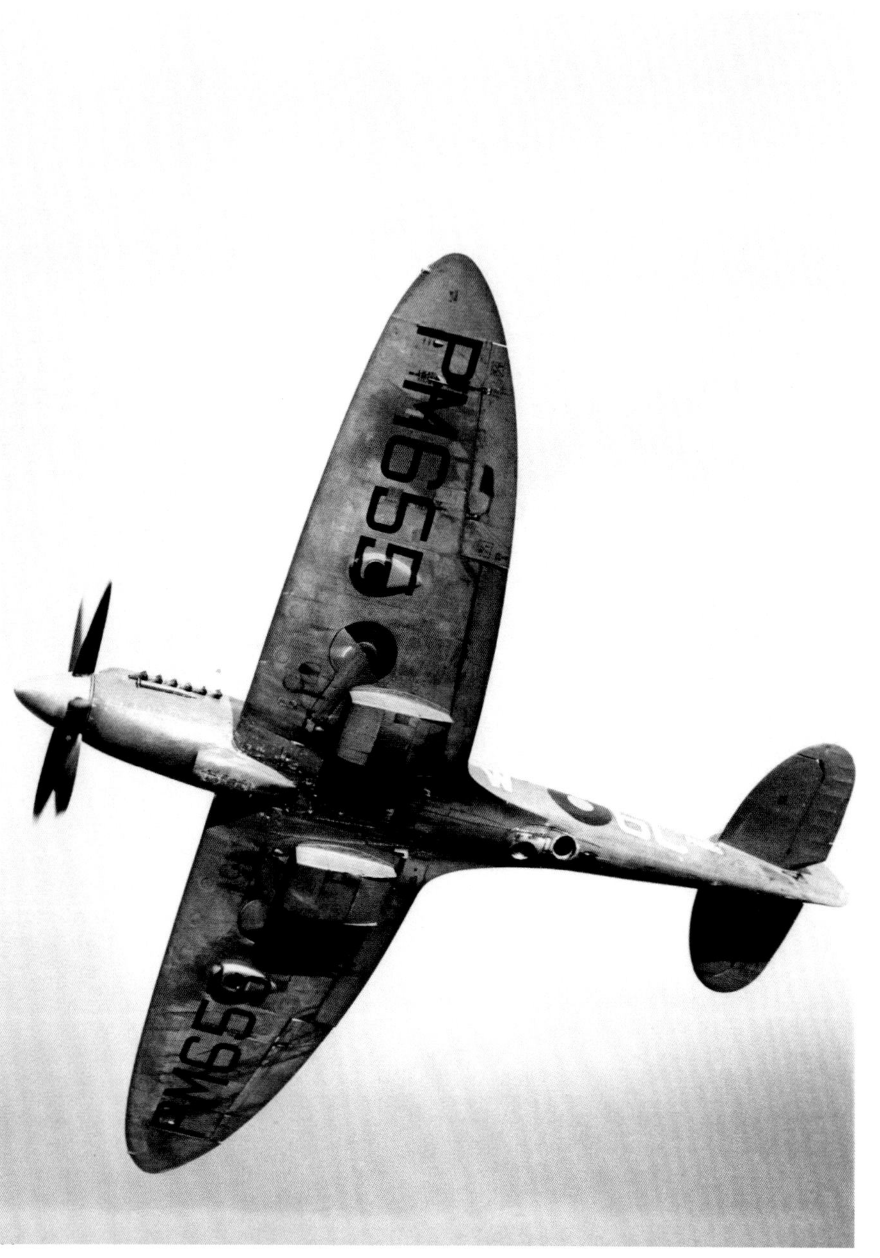

Spitfire PR Mk XIX, PM655 '6C-W', of the RAF Air Photographic Development Unit during Operation 'Revue', the extensive aerial photographic survey of Britain, April 1950. Although superceded by jet fighters, Spitfires continued to be used in RAF service well into the 1950s.

Aerial cameras being removed from Spitfire PR Mk XIX PS890 of 81 Squadron during the Malayan Emergency. The Mk XIX was the only photo reconaissance variant powered by the Griffon engine and was the type that carried out the RAF's final operational Spitfire flight on 1 April 1954.

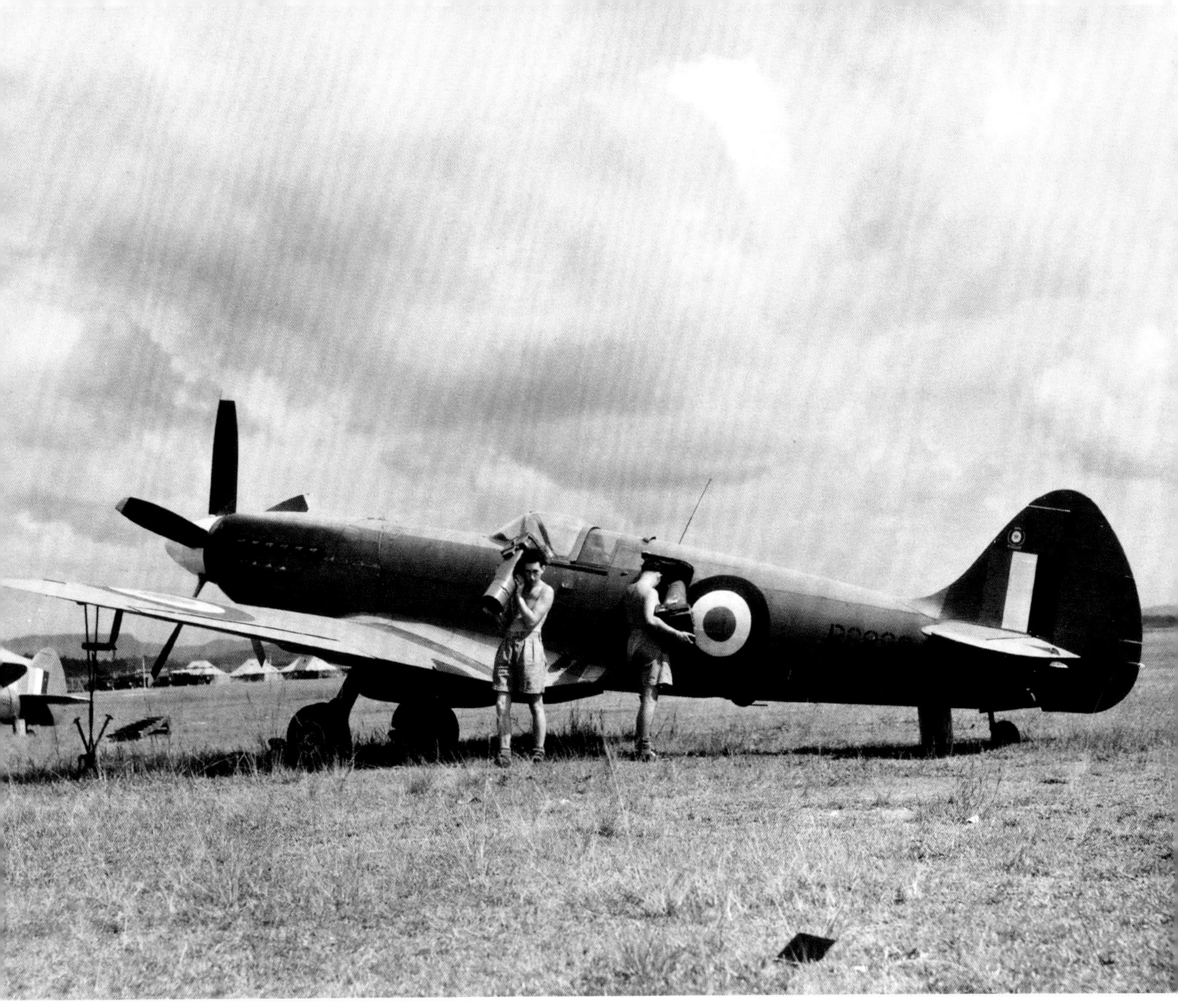

The last of the RAF's Spitfires in 'vic' formation en route to their retirement at Biggin Hill, July 1957. Along with one Hawker Hurricane, these PR Mk XIX Spitfires formed what is now known as the Battle of Britain Memorial Flight (crop).

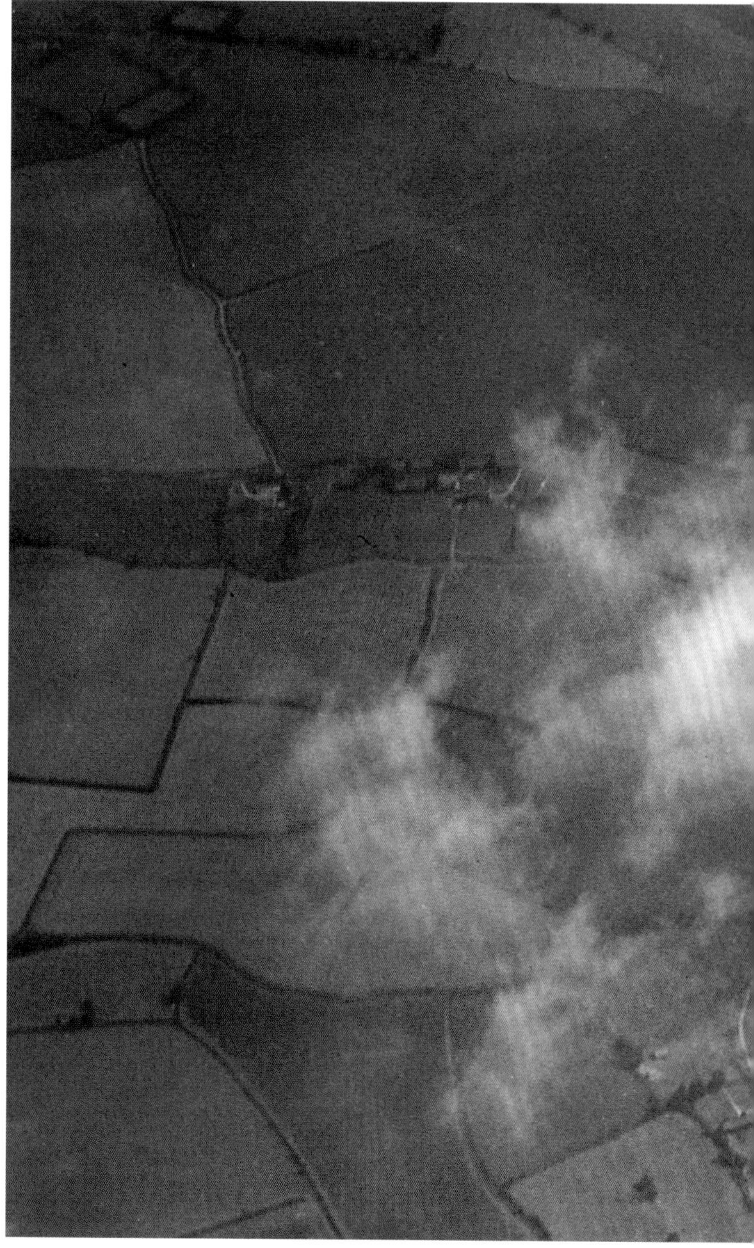

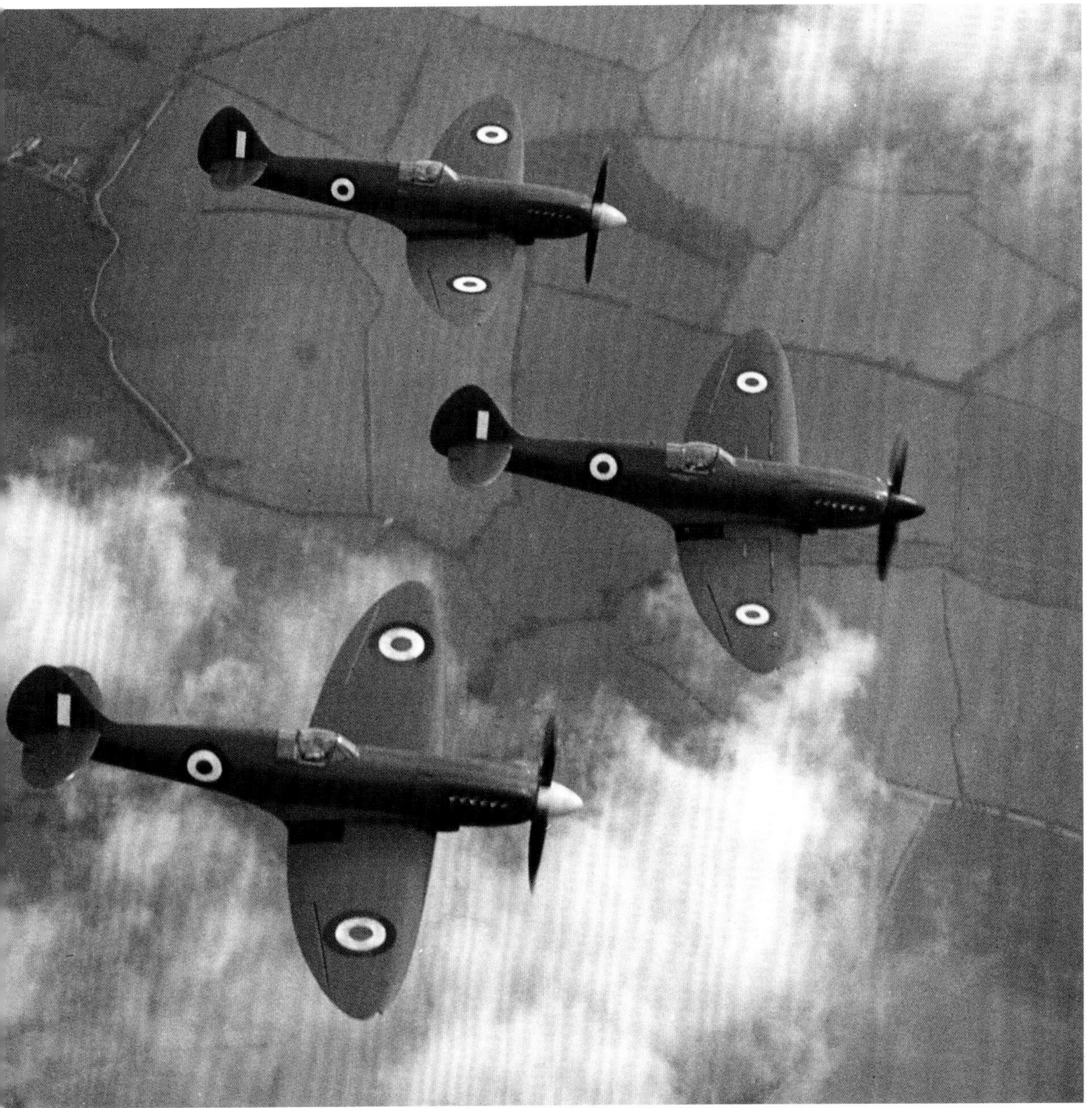

Image List

HU 1659, CH 19, HU 48148, HU 104747, HU 104745, HU 86061, CH 741, CH 1367, TR 139, COL 207, CH 4180, CH 2929, HU 140539, CH 5291, COL 189 (cropped), CAN 278, TR 865, TR 1066, CNA 2272, CNA 2102, CH 18083, HU 88209, TR 513, CH 18603, TR 1531, CH 12890, CL 108, HU 92143, CL 1450, IND 3182, CNA 2829, CNA 3175, CF 682, CF 660, CH 12751, CH 12753, CH 12754, E(MOS) 1325, CH 13814, CH 13817, MH 6848, FE 599, CL 1698, HU 1681, HU 1682, HU 57727, HU 57732, HU 64726, HU 140540, HU 140541

About the Author

Adrian Kerrison has worked as a Curator in IWM's Second World War and Mid-20th Century Conflict team since 2016 and is based at IWM Duxford. He has curated several exhibitions, including *Hangar 4 Battle of Britain* at IWM Duxford and *Spitfire: Evolution of an Icon.*

Acknowledgements

The author would like to thank the following IWM colleagues for their support: John Delaney and Chris Cooper (Joint Heads of the Second World War and Mid-20th Century Conflict team), Madeleine James (Publishing & Brand Licensing Manager) and Helen Mavin (Head of Photographs), as well as the many other colleagues involved in publishing this book. Thank you as well to my parents for kicking off my lifelong interest in this subject by taking me to IWM Duxford as a child, and to my wife Isabel for her unwavering support.